Water Gardens

Step by Step to Growing Success

Brian Leverett

W9-BKI-562

First Published in 1990 by
The Crowood Press Ltd
Ramsbury, Marlborough
Wiltshire SN8 2HR

© The Crowood Press 1990 and 1996

Revised edition 1996

All rights reserved. No part of this publication may be
reproduced or transmitted in any form or by any means,
electrical or mechanical, including photocopy, record-
ing, or any information storage and retrieval system,
without the permission in writing from the publishers.

British Library Cataloguing in Publication Data
A catalogue record for this publication is available from
the British Library.

ISBN 1 85223 977 8

Picture Credits
With acknowledgements to Bruce Grant-Braham, Ken-
nedy's Garden Centre, Geoff Moore of Dorset Media
Services, Dave Pike, Yvonne Rees, Jan and Frank Tay-
lor, all remaining pictures supplied by the author who is
indebted to Dr R. Page and R. Newman MSc.

Colour artwork by Claire Upsdale-Jones.

Dedication
To Ann, whose garden inspired this book.

Typeset and designed by
D & N Publishing
Ramsbury, Marlborough
Wiltshire SN8 2HR

Typeface used: Plantin.

Imagesetting by Dorwyn Ltd, Chichester.

Printed and bound by Paramount Printing, Hong Kong.

Contents

Introduction

Walk into any garden and it is the water which catches the eye: whether it is a cascading waterfall, a fountain or darting fishes the movement coupled with the magic that is water makes it the area which attracts attention. It is impossible to say why we are so fascinated by water; it's as though there were something in our primitive past which has created a bond between it and man. As children we sought out ponds as areas of special interest; and when we develop our own gardens it seems an indispensable feature. No garden is complete without water.

CREATING A NATURAL ENVIRONMENT

The gardener comes nearer to creating a natural environment in the water garden than in any other part of the cultivated plot, and like all natural environments there are few sharp lines of division but rather gradual changes as we move from the deep water with its water-lilies and fishes, through the shallows and marginal plants, to the bog garden of saturated soil.

In the natural world different species have evolved to exploit wet habitats with the number and range of species increasing as the water becomes shallower. It is amongst the bogland plants – those that require sodden soil rather than deep water – that the greatest variety is found. Some plants are tolerant of a wide range of conditions and will grow as bedding plants, providing that they are watered frequently and never allowed to dry out. But they will never give of their best unless we provide them

A layout incorporating both classical and natural elements in a green colour scheme (opposite).

with ideal conditions, which are often to be found only around the water garden.

As well as water, wetland habitats usually consist of impoverished soil as the water leeches out the soluble nutrients. Plants that grow in such conditions are used to struggling to survive, needing to fight for a living, but even in the harshest ecosystems there must always be the occasional provision of nutrients, through entry of decaying

An attractive irregular pond well stocked with water-lilies.

A general view of a water garden in late summer.

material. The gardener improves upon these haphazard windfalls by lifting, propagating or regenerating to stimulate the plant, and replanting in soil enriched with controlled amounts of well-rotted manure.

As with all gardening, the key to success is to create an environment that imitates nature, yet at the same time managing a resource in such a manner that you obtain the best possible results; we cannot improve on nature but we can make the best use of what it provides. You will never deceive nature – you cannot cultivate in a way that it does not allow – but you can manipulate the natural world to serve your purpose, bringing together plants from a variety of locations around the world into your small corner of suburbia.

POND ENVIRONMENT

Responsible Management

Water gardening is the creation of a special environment, which holds more than just horticultural interest. Animals and insects will visit your pond and perhaps colonize it, whether you wish them to or not. The visit by a dragonfly is far more transient than the stay of the water-lily, but it is as much part of the total beauty of the pond on a summer's day. The unpredictability of its appearance adds to its exclusivity and mystery. For far too long we sought to kill insects, often not bothering to distinguish between those that were genuinely harmful and those that were beneficial. Many were driven to the edge of extinction. The gradual decrease in predatory insects – those that controlled the numbers of garden pests – led to a need for even greater use of the once virtually non-selective pesticides. For a while it seemed that farms and private gardens were addicted to these chemical killers. But fortunately attitudes changed as man became better educated to the needs of his environment and moved to adopt a far more responsible approach. Today we seek to solve problems by using the minimum amount of (usually) selective pesticides, actively seeking to encourage the predators back into the garden in order that they can naturally control the numbers of pests: the integrated approach to gardening.

Fortunately, insect life is resilient, and so few insects became extinct as a result of man's interference. With the modern approach – in which we work with nature rather than against it – we can contain problems using natural agencies to control pests, together with only the minimum amount of chemicals.

A colourful pool with Higoi carp.

The Garden Pond and Conservation

At the same time that an excess of chemicals were being used to control pests, the countryside was being covered with concrete, destroying precious habitats. Such creatures as the beautiful dragonflies, which had escaped the worst of the chemical attacks, were now threatened through loss of habitat as ponds were drained and built upon. Nomadic creatures, they require a network of ponds to ensure their survival, and it seems likely that the salvation of these most spectacular of insects, together with the amphibians – frogs, toads and newts – will be the many new garden ponds, insignificant on their own, but together forming a potent force for conservation. The vast areas of private garden in the UK hold the potential to become a vast nature reserve and guarantee the survival of species.

Water gardening is totally environmentally friendly. The only insect pests likely to be encountered – aphids – may be removed simply by spraying the plants with a jet of water. Falling into the pond, they then serve to satisfy part of the fishes' voracious appetites. Ponds provide the start to a whole range of food chains, which will help restore the balance of nature whilst at the same time introducing some of the most interesting creatures into the garden.

Avoiding Problems

Gardeners are always part artist, part naturalist and part scientist, and nowhere is this description more accurate than in the water garden. The misuse of science has created large-scale problems, yet a lack

ENVIRONMENTAL ADVANTAGES OF A WATER GARDEN

- ❀ Provides a diversity of habitat which attracts a wide range of species into the garden, many of them feeding on pests. The greater the range of species, the more readily the balance of nature is restored.
- ❀ Provides a home for frogs, which feed extensively on slugs, snails and other pests.
- ❀ Provides a home for toads, which consume large numbers of ants and other pests.
- ❀ Provides a water supply for the several species of birds that feed on pests, which are in many cases at the larval stage before they are capable of reproducing.
- ❀ Provides a water supply for bees and other pollinating insects.
- ❀ Most importantly it provides a restful, stress-free environment where humans can temporarily escape from the pressures of the modern world.

of knowledge of basic botany is probably the most frequent cause of failure in most gardens. To avoid the problems which result from ignorance, the underlying principles of plant growth and cultivation have been included in the text. The information should be sufficient for the general reader, but for greater detail on plants and animals you are strongly advised to consult specialist reference books. You will find the extra knowledge rewarding in itself, and it will enhance your enjoyment of the garden.

WATER IN GARDEN DESIGN

The use of water in creating gardens is very old, having been practised since classical times. The Romans, who were great garden builders, brought the ideas of the Mediterranean to the lands which they conquered and made, amongst other features, lead ponds. However, the ideas for water gardening as we know it today almost certainly originated from Renaissance Europe. In the Seventeenth and Eighteenth centuries, elaborate water gardens were to be constructed in the vast estates of the wealthy. Water was to become one of the most important elements in English classical landscaping incorporated into the designs of many of the great parklands.

A gazebo provides both a scenic background, and will also function as a shed or storage room for tools.

The shape of the pond together with its immediate surroundings determines the effect that it creates.

A pond, whether large or small, is an integral part of the garden.

Modern gardening requires a totally different approach to that adopted for large country houses, and yet it is clear that the water garden is as important an integral part of the overall design of the small garden as it is of the large. Today we realize that size is not the most important factor, although the larger the available area the more you can achieve. Where there is room for a flowerbed there is space for a water garden. However, such a garden must be designed with water in mind, with the other features made to fit around it. Ponds may account for most of the garden plot, they may be the central feature of a larger scheme, or they may be effectively separated from the rest of the plot. All

Plan the water garden in terms of the garden as a whole, designing the total layout before commencement of work.

A pond carefully sited in a woodland setting.

BEWARE

❀ Correctly used water is perfectly safe, but it is potentially a killer and must be treated with respect.

❀ Just a few inches of water is enough to drown someone – especially children: young children should never be allowed to play unsupervised near a pond.

❀ Water and electricity are a lethal combination: exposed wires or incorrect connections can lead to a fatal shock. Installation should be made by a competent professional; it is not a task for an enthusiastic Do-It-Yourselfer.

❀ Water is extremely heavy: each gallon weighs 10 pounds (4.5kg). A pond included as part of a roof garden puts a great strain on the roof, and such structures should be designed and built only by professionals who have adequate experience and insurance cover.

sizes and shapes can be accommodated and any thoughts of failure can be dismissed, providing that the creator studies and understands the subject, rather than rushing out spade in hand to dig a hole. For example if fish are to be kept it is necessary to appreciate the amount of room they require, their enemies, their feeding requirements, and their need for oxygen and how it is to be provided.

Just as it can be said that water is needed to complete a garden, it is never an end in itself; it is at its most effective where it will bring out the best in other garden features and where they in turn will make the most of the water. Water fits into every type of design from the classical or formal styles to the geometric designs of patio gardens and the decorated approach in which statuettes, windmills and other man-made features are included to complete the scene. If good water gardening is one of the finest features of the garden, nothing is quite as bad as water poorly used. The role of water must be very carefully planned for whilst it is possible to fit water into every type of garden, this does not mean that water can be included in every position. A small pond fitted into a rock garden almost as though it were an additional plant providing a type of ground cover does not work. Water and rocks both possess an ageless character, so they go well together, and some of the best designs for water gardens incorporate the use of rocks; but the balance of the two features is very important. They must appear to live in harmony, with neither tending to dominate the other.

Modern pond liners and moulds are excellent, involving less work, expense and skill to site than the older concrete ponds, but where their presence is seen the whole effect is destroyed. A water garden should either appear to be a perfectly natural part of the environment (as though nature itself had laid it out), or clearly a man-made creation in what is plainly a totally artificial environment.

CHAPTER 1

Siting the Water Garden

The most important consideration, which must be correctly resolved before any construction work is attempted, is the position of your proposed water garden. Although the water garden has its own special demands, it must be planned in terms of the garden as a whole. The garden layout you choose

The water garden is an essential feature of the larger plot.

When planning a water garden it is advisable to work out the advantages of the various sites on paper first.

will dictate the position and, to some extent, the shape and size of the pool, and the water feature most harmonious with the overall scheme in all respects. Should you choose to make water the central theme of your garden, or a part of the garden which is separated by a screen or other visual obstruction, the whole area must be designed in such a way that an aesthetic balance is created.

The water garden must have adequate sunlight. This is needed to penetrate the water and allow the water weeds to perform photosynthesis in order to maintain the dissolved oxygen level in the water. Green algae is sometimes said to grow solely as a result of a pond receiving too much sunlight, but this is not correct, for it thrives where there is an excess of nutrients and an absence of predators to live off it. It is, therefore, the result of a poor environmental balance. The water garden should also be protected as far as possible from the worst effects of easterly and westerly winds, otherwise the plants may become damaged or broken, or at the very least suffer from wind burn, where the extremities of the leaves turn brown, then black, before falling off.

The factors affecting the siting of a water garden are the same whether it is to be a new feature in an established garden, or the whole garden is being designed for the first time. Before embarking on any plan you must study the climatic conditions and see how they affect your garden; ignoring this could result in

A pond may be constructed in a wooded area and where there are hedges providing that shadows are not thrown over the pond for any length of time during the day and that leaves are not allowed to enter the water.

IDENTIFYING A SITE

In narrowing down the possible sites for your water garden:
1. Omit all the areas where it is impractical to build the feature, such as a front open-plan garden which may be liable to damage by dogs, or areas which are hidden from view.
2. Draw a scale plan of the whole, marking the areas which are in shade and which should be avoided. The length of shadow that any object will throw should be appreciated. It may not be possible to find a position which is totally free of all shadows, but you should look for the position which enjoys the maximum amount of daily sunlight. In this respect the effect of trees should also be carefully considered, for apart from the problems of leaves falling they may throw a shadow across part or all of the pond.
3. Establish the true north of the garden. Mark it clearly on the diagram and include the directions of the prevailing winds. The intensity of the winds will depend very much on the position of the garden. If you are situated in an exposed location, near to the sea or on the side of a steep hill, you will suffer far stronger effects of wind than if you are in a valley.
4. Identify possible frost traps and sunspots. Valleys will often act as frost traps, but this slight difference in temperature is unlikely to be sufficient to cause problems. Every area has microclimates which may be considerably different from the area as a whole. There will also be degrees of microclimate within any one country – a county on the western seaboard will have a far wetter climate than the rest of the country, while coasts washed by the Gulf Stream will have a warmer climate than would be expected for the latitude. Consequently, those towns nearer the water will usually be at higher temperatures than land-locked towns in the same county. Within the town itself there will be different climatic conditions, depending on the degree of exposure or the nearness of the buildings which may be emitting their own heat. Within the garden itself there will be hot spots (such as against a south-facing wall), while exposed positions may be vulnerable to frosts, receiving them earlier in the year, and of a greater intensity in winter.
5. When deciding the best possible site, you need to choose the point from which you will most frequently observe the water garden, perhaps from a window in the house. If the garden fronts on to the street, you may wish to create the view so that the passer-by derives the maximum benefit. It is possible to design a garden where the view is virtually the same from the house and the street, more so with the formal symmetrical pond than with the informal system, because in the latter the taller subjects need to be placed to the back of the pond.

expensive failure. However, ponds do not require perfect conditions and pampering, and there is a degree of latitude on most sites that allows for a choice of positions.

ELEVATIONS

With all but the simplest planting schemes there will be differences in height and, looking across the garden from the main vantage point, the furthermost part will be elevated compared with the flat level of the pond. Such high levels should ideally be at the northern boundary of the plot having a southerly aspect, but plots are seldom constructed with a simple north-south elevation, and tend to lie between the cardinal points of the compass. Where it is impossible to obtain an exactly south-facing site it is best either to get as near to a southerly aspect as possible, or to use an easterly aspect

(where it will be necessary to give careful consideration to the effects of the wind). The soil itself takes a large amount of heat from the atmosphere to warm up just a few degrees, and is also a poor conductor of heat. As a consequence of the high heat capacity, the deeper you go into the ground the less the temperature changes as a result of the seasons, and heat (or lack of it) at the earth's surface. This is particularly important to the pond builder, because at the bottom of a deepish pond there will be water that is less susceptible to change. Although it will slowly rise to the surface by convection currents and be subjected to the heat losses at this point, it effectively stops the water from freezing completely, except in the severest winters. The water can freeze solid when ponds are built above ground level. In certain protected areas, or where there is a favourable microclimate, such ponds will present no problems in most years, but during the very severe winters that occur from time

The small water garden with running water may be situated on most sites.
It has a charm and beauty all of its own.

to time, the possibility of the water freezing solid with the total loss of the animal pond life, cannot be ruled out.

Windbreaks

Where wind is a particular problem it will be necessary to construct a windbreak. Walls and solid fences effectively provide protection to a distance of about three times their height from the wall itself. At midday, when the sun is at its most intense, the length of the shadow will be equal to the height of the wall, so clearly there is an area which will receive a maximum amount of sunlight and which will still be afforded protection from the wind. A hedge is a better windbreak than a solid wall, which only deflects the wind to some other position. A hedge, fence or screen in which there are gaps, breaks up the air current, offering the maximum protection while not concentrating the air to form a strong draught. Moreover, a hedge often blends into the overall garden design far better than a wall.

SIZE

In some gardens the size of the area which can be given over to the water garden will be restricted, but even in modern high-density estate developments there is always room to construct a whole water garden with marginals and bogs. Where there is a restriction on size, it is better to build a larger pond and to omit the bog garden, and even if necessary to reduce the margins, rather than try to get too much into a confined space. The smallest practical size for a pond is about 6ft (180cm) by 4ft (120cm). It is possible to construct smaller ponds, and they can give you much pleasure for raising plants, keeping fish and attracting wildlife, but at that size they are not a landscape feature and are better thought of as outdoor aquariums. The larger the pond the fewer problems it will create and the wider the range of wildlife it will attract. Ponds require a depth of at least 2ft (60cm); this extra depth is needed not only for water-lilies to grow, but to accommodate the fish during cold winter spells, and to reduce the likelihood of the pond freezing solid. Regardless of the surface area, always ensure that you have this depth of water. (An outdoor aquarium is an exception to this rule, which need not apply if you intend only to grow miniature water-lilies. However, the reduced size may restrict the growth of any goldfish you may wish to include.)

A small water garden should not be thought of in terms of miniaturization of a large aquascape, but rather as an individual design, tailor-made for the space that is available.

THE GARDEN PLAN

Having decided the possible sites from a climatic point of view and the limitations imposed by the size of the plot, you need to decide which of the suitable positions (there will almost certainly be more than one) is the best in terms of the overall garden design. You could plan your overall garden design, with the water garden provisionally 'pencilled in', and then decide whether there are any problems in terms of climate, and whether you could resolve them by the use of windbreaks or other appropriate structures. Whichever approach you use, it is important that the water garden is seen as part of the whole and its broader role in the garden design is appreciated from the outset. Never start building a water garden or any part of the garden until you have fully planned the whole plot. Decide the theme of your garden and then design the water garden accordingly. There are six main styles of garden.

The Formal Garden

The formal garden is based on symmetry, and the elements that make it up have straight, sharp edges

Here, height is created with a built-up rockery area and the surrounding plants chosen to create balance.

with rigid right angles. They may alternatively be designed based on a circle or oval if the overall plan demands it. Total harmony will exist between all of the features: there will be well-tended beds, laid out in geometrical patterns, and immaculate lawns with sharp edges. Think very carefully before incorporating more than a pond in such a design as, although a margin will not necessarily appear irregular, many of the marginal plants are not of the type to blend in with a fully formal garden design. Moreover the flowers will tend to be overshadowed by those in the borders or by the roses (a popular feature of formal gardens), both of which are dominant in their impact. Ponds for formal gardens will normally be of rectangular or square shape, reflecting the shape of the garden as a whole, and flagstones are laid at the edge for the sharp angles that are the important feature. Where formal gardens are based

on the use of curves and arcs, round or oval-shaped ponds are constructed to mimic the overall shape.

The pond should be situated at the centre of the plot to produce a perfectly balanced overall design – a formal garden always has a centre or plane of symmetry which acts as a focal point. Water-lilies, with their bold, almost rose-like global flowers, are the only plants that blend totally into formal system. Because of the harmony that exists between the water-lily and the rose, rose gardens, which are usually constructed as a special type of formal garden, are particularly suited to the inclusion of a regularly shaped pond as a centrepiece. Where water-lilies are used in a formal setting they should be replanted from time to time to ensure that no more than one-third of the surface area of water is covered with the floating leaves. (It may be necessary to allow an increase in coverage if algae growth is a

A formal fountain and pool.

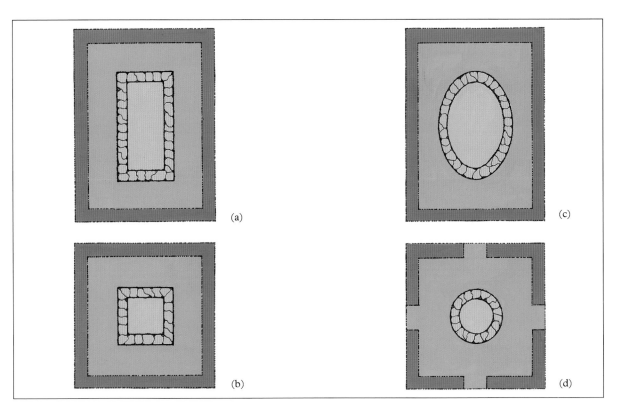

Layout of ponds into a formal garden. (a) With a rectangular plot the pond should be of the same proportions as the plot itself; (b) totally formal but nevertheless a style which is always in fashion – the square pond inside the square plot; (c) an oval pond with the proportion of the maximum to minimum axes the same as that of the side of the plot; (d) the pure curves of the circle are capable of balancing the sharp angles and equal sides of the square. **Note:** *You should never place a rectangular pond in a square garden or vice versa; never place an oval or rectangular shape contrary to the direction of the plot; in a formal garden the pond must harmonize with the plot.*

problem.) The irregular growth of irises should also be avoided. Formal gardens are not intended to appear natural, but are an art form in which the gardener is always in complete command.

The plan of the garden will dictate the position of the pond. Formal gardens demand an open, sunny aspect, to show off to the best advantage the bright colours and design features. The only visible pond plants will be the water-hugging lilies, and they will be less prone to wind damage than higher-growing subjects would. It may be assumed that any location that is suitable for a formal garden may successfully accommodate a pond.

The Informal Garden

Paradoxically, the informal garden is also completely planned, and always under the control of its creator. The effect is intended, however, to be more 'natural', with the lines being softer, to give the impression that nature is in command. Such gardens allow for more latitude, and it is here that the complete water garden can be created. The initial impression is one of the shapes and details created by the vegetation, and water and rocks are such natural subjects for inclusion into such scenes. There are two main types of informal garden in which water may be included, the cottage garden and the rock garden.

Sysyrinchium brachypus, *a hardy, tufted, iris-like plant.*

The Cottage Garden

This often looks simply like a disoriented patch in which old-fashioned flowers are grown, but in fact it also requires planning around a simple theme. There are usually herbaceous or mixed beds con-taining a variety of shrubs, annuals and perennials, and the casual, apparently carefree effect belies the meticulous attention to detail which has gone into their creation. In such gardens water may be the main theme, passing through all the depths until all

Marginal planting.

that remain are the dry plant beds. Alternatively, if climatic factors demand, the water garden may be situated at one of the sides or, if the aspect dictates, in one of the corners. The demands of the water garden may be allowed to take precedence over all others, and this type of design encourages the inclusion of all shapes and shades of plant growth, and the greatest variety of pond marginals and bog plants.

The principle of planning terrestrial beds is well understood, and the same rules can be applied to water garden designs. Such a feature is seldom studied at short range, but more frequently viewed from a distance, and the observer should be able to take in all the organic and inorganic characteristics with a sweep of his eyes.

Remember that an informal pond design is unlikely to present a similar view from all points of the compass, so you must decide which part of the pond you wish to be considered the 'front'. Do not neglect the other views though: the pond should be planned so that it presents an interesting view from all vantage points, albeit that one or two may afford the greater interest.

One of the commonest faults in many water gardens with a good selection of marginals and bog plants is that taller subjects, such as irises, are at the very front of the pond, obscuring the rest of the plants from view.

The planting scheme for all the plants involved will need to be plotted out on a plan of the water garden, with the largest subjects at the back, and the small upright plants progressively further and further to the front. Water-lilies, with their low-growing habit, will perform a role similar to that of the pansy in the herbaceous bed. Either all the taller-growing subjects can be to the back, or there may be a gradual lessening of the height along the side, with an empty open area at the front of the pond, so that the water-lilies may be seen from the original designated vantage point.

Due regard must be given to the position of the garden relative to the points of the compass. For example, if the pond is on the south side of the property because of the restrictions imposed by the vantage point, then the tall subjects cannot be planted at the back. Instead, the water needs an open aspect down the centre of its concourse, in

A natural-looking waterfall.

A watercourse amongst a rockery with stones of the district remains one of the most difficult layouts to improve upon.

order that the water-lilies receive the maximum amount of sunlight. Plant the pond and marginals down the sides, but retain the principle of the tallest being away from the observer.

The Rock Garden

Water and stone both have great age, and together they produce an effect that gives a sense of time-lessness to a garden. Virtually all ponds have some stone or concrete associated with them. In the rock garden pond, part of the land surrounding the water is raised and used to construct a rock or alpine gar-den. In many senses the rock garden which needs good drainage to grow alpines – which draw the water they need from the thin film of moisture adhering by surface tension to the underside of the stones – is the reverse of a water garden. However, they do work well together if you carefully select the alpine subjects which survive most conditions, pro-viding their roots are dry. By combining both a rock and water garden it is possible to achieve one of the most natural looking of landscapes, but although the two blend together from a horticultural point of view, it is best to consider the rock garden and the pool as separate entities, where both are planted and maintained independently.

There is another important advantage to including a rock garden with a pond: constructing the pond will produce a great deal of spoilage in the form of top soil, and large amounts of work and the problems associated with redepositing it can be avoided by using it to create a rockery to the rear of the pool. This will give the garden more than one level, with plant height ranging from the floating lily pads to the tallest alpine. Concentrated into the small space of a modern garden, all this will give the area a sense of mass.

So there are very strong arguments for creating a rock garden in conjunction with a water garden. If this approach appeals to you, not only should the whole garden be designed before any work is attempted, but also the fine detail should be worked out, such as the quantity of rock required. Order it all at the same time, so that even if it is not possible to do all the work at once, the rock will match throughout. It may also be cheaper to buy a single load of stone, which will involve just one journey from the quarry.

Rodgersia pinnata.

Classical Gardens

Within a relatively small plot (but perhaps not in a really tiny modern estate garden) it is possible to create a classical style garden, which takes its inspiration from the Seventeenth and Eighteenth century landscaped designs. Here the emphasis is not on bright colours – virtually all of the visual effect is created by green, including all shades, from the dark green of privet, through the medium green of a lawn, to the almost yellow-green of certain cultivars or shrubs. The main harmonizing colour is the grey white of limestone which makes up the pond. Bright coloured flowers are used extremely cautiously, but include daffodils in spring, summer favourites such as antirrhinum, and Michaelmas daisies for the autumn. The eye is instinctively drawn towards these and care must be taken to ensure that they do not predominate and take over the scene. The garden depends very much upon the form of the trees and shrubs (their height, mass and shape) creating a living organic sculpture, a constantly changing scene. The pondscape and structure provide the only element that is not dependent upon the seasons of the year.

There is a degree of latitude in the shaping of the pond, which may be either round, or of an asymmetrical shape. The important factor is to use stone which has aged since it was cut and dressed to give a totally natural appearance. You may find such stone on a demolition site, and it is well worth rescuing as well as cheaper than the fresh-cut material. Accessories, in the form of reproduction classical sculptures or fountains, may be included in the design. Do ensure, however, that they are made of a material that will blend with that of the pond surrounds. Do not spoil the effect by using obviously cheap and inferior plastic models.

Ornamental Gardens

In an ornamental garden a large number of accessories are used to give a certain feel to the plot. Such gardens cover an enormous range, from Baroque or even Rococo, to the ubiquitous garden gnomes, but whatever your taste water will almost certainly find its way in. The pond, which can be of any shape, may be kept relatively simple. The plants are secondary to the artefacts and little beyond water-lilies need be grown. Marginals will represent a further complication, tending to detract from the inorganics. The pond and rocks may be the only permanent features in an area which will change with the whim of fashion – windmills, bridges and similar features will allow the creator to display his woodworking skills.

The Patio

The origins of patio gardening are very old indeed, and the name is derived from the Spanish for 'courtyard'. It is only in recent years that the approach has become very popular with urban gardeners, and a sizeable part of the fast-growing garden-centre trade has been directed towards the patio gardener. With its less demanding calls on space and time of the owner, patio gardening is tailor-made for the modern life-style. Perhaps more than any other type of garden, a patio

A totally modern approach in this pond which is set amongst paving stones and patio slabs.

demands the use of water, to provide necessary variety in a visual sense to break up the stonework. However, the styles of water garden that are appropriate are strictly limited. In general the patio lends itself to a geometrical, usually rectangular type of pool (most conveniently constructed from either liners or fibreglass moulds). Using concrete it is possible to make two modest pools, interconnected with 4in (10cm) pipe. Alternatively, an overlap of 4in (10cm) of the patio slabs may be provided, where the fish will shelter. Where the patio itself is constructed on two levels a waterfall may be included, with the water cascading from the upper level. The visual effect, together with the sound, will accentuate the differences in height. Each pool may be made to suit different types of water-lily, but generally a shallower structure is favourable. No fountain should produce a jet of more than about 24in (60cm). It is important to keep everything in proportion in the small courtyard-type layout.

Within all garden designs there will be a natural place for water, but including this element you must ensure that it harmonizes, reflecting the features of the other parts of the design. Remember always that the design must be very carefully considered – it is far easier to move the features around on paper than it is to manhandle soils and rocks. To get a better idea of the visual effect of the water garden, mark out the shape of the pond in the position that it is to occupy with 3ft (1m) rods. Examine the result from all positions including, importantly, from your most likely vantage point in the house, considering the view of your garden which you will most frequently see. Change the position of the rods until you are completely satisfied with the effect, then permanently mark out the area to be occupied by the pond.

SURROUNDS FOR FORMAL POOLS

paving stones

bricks

bricks

crazy paving

bricks

patio blocks

With formal designs, including those for the patio, there is a vast range of possibilities offered by the surrounds. As long as the design of the surround is symmetrical and in keeping with the pool itself, designs can range from the very simple to the complex and intricate.

CHAPTER 2

Building the Pond

Natural ponds do occur in some gardens but they are relatively rare, usually in association with a layer of clay near to the surface. This layer effectively stops the water from escaping and, providing that it acts as part of a natural drainage system and sufficient rainfall is received, it will maintain a relatively constant level, creating what is, perhaps, the best pond of all. Apart from construction, natural ponds may be considered similar in every way to the man-made equivalent. In order to create move-ment a second, artificial pond, above the level of the natural one, may be created.

In the vast majority of instances, however, there will be no natural pond, and the gardener will have to construct one. There are three basic ways of doing this – with concrete, with a liner, or with a fibreglass mould.

Rocks and water complement each other very well, as seen here where a rockery has been built up on one side of the pool.

ESSENTIALS OF A WELL-DESIGNED POND

1. The largest possible surface area.
This will ensure that the maximum gaseous exchange can occur, thus allowing the largest quantity of fish life to be kept. A pond 3 feet by 3 feet by a foot deep contains 9 cu. feet of water as does one which is 3 feet long by a foot wide by 3 feet deep. However, the second pond will support far less life than the first as the area for gaseous exchange is only a third of that of the former. Fish will not survive in a pond which is totally shallow, and so it is necessary to incorporate a deep trough for the fish to live in during the winter.

2. The greatest possible variation in depth.
To rear fish you require three depths. The first, 3–5ft (1–1½m), will serve as a retreat for fish in very cold weather and is also necessary to grow several varieties of water-lily. The second depth consists of varying shallow areas of 1–1½ft (30–45cm) for the growing of oxygenating plants. These latter depths can be achieved by gently sloping sides or shelves. The third depth is an intermediate area between the two where fish can rest during the active season.

SIZE

As a general rule the larger the pond the better the results, because bringing together several species of plants and animals into a confined space will result in the stronger destroying the weaker; for the same reason population levels of both must be carefully managed.

ORGANIZING THE WORK

Pond building involves a great deal of physical work and requires the movement of a large quantity of top soil, so before any work is started you must plan where the soil is to be placed. If it is good quality loam, soil may be used for a raised structure such as a rock garden. Before transporting the soil large distances, remember that a rock and water garden combined is a very attractive visual feature, far more effective than two distinct entities in different parts of the garden. When moving soil, take the top fertile layer away and place it to one side before moving away any subsoil which lacks the humus to maintain plant life. Ensure that the fertile soil is returned to the top of any structure built from excavated earth. Often ponds are constructed in lawns in which it is intended to retain the lawn after the water garden has been built. To protect the grass, cover the area where any subsoil is to be deposited with a tarpaulin or heavy-duty plastic sheeting, avoiding materials that tear easily as they may be subjected to rough treatment. Transporting rocks to the site and soil away from it will require a wheelbarrow, and the heavy weight on the wheel can result in a ridge being cut in the lawn. Avoid the problem by placing planks on the lawn to form a track over which the barrow may be pushed.

THE CONCRETE POND

In many respects concrete is the best material for making ponds, and for may years was the only one available. Today it is the most expensive, and for even the smallest pond considerably more physical work in terms of moving and mixing cement and sand is involved than in other methods – where even a modest size of pond is contemplated it may well pay to hire a cement mixer. The cost is the major disadvantage of the method. Thick, strong sides to the pond are necessary to withstand the forces created and the effects of freezing, and a 4in (10cm) concrete wall is the thinnest which can be relied upon to perform the task. If you are considering using concrete it is advisable to calculate the quantity and cost of materials at the outset.

DECIDING WHICH BUILDING MATERIALS TO USE

1. Determine the size and shape of the pond.
2. Decide whether there is any danger of the membrane being punctured.
3. Consider your ability to do the work: concrete pools are the most difficult to lay, followed by glass-fibre moulds; plastic sheeting is the easiest.
4. Calculate the cost of the materials. Concrete ponds are the most expensive, then fibre-glass, liners are the cheapest.

Dimensions

Rectangular Pond

In imperial units To build a pond 4in (⅓ft) thick. Measure the width (W), depth (D) and breadth (B). The addition is made to include the volume necessary to create the floor of the pond. The result will be in cubic feet – to convert to cubic yards, divide by 27.

$$([2W \times D] + [2B \times D]) \times \tfrac{1}{3} + (W \times B \times \tfrac{1}{3})$$

Where the pond is to be of varying depths, such as where a shelf is to be constructed for marginals, the calculation must be modified to take this into account. The effect of the step will be equivalent to a shortfall, produced as a lack of depth at the shallow end, and the calculation in respect of the breadth will remain the same for both ends. The difference will occur in the sides, which should each be considered as two components, made up of two distinct lengths and depths. Should you wish to create the pond at three distinct levels (which might be necessary if you intend to grow a range of plants which require different water depths), you will need to perform the calculation employing three distinct components for the item.

Example The amount of concrete needed to build a rectangular pond 9 × 6ft, to a depth of 2ft for two-thirds of the length and a depth of 6in for the remaining third, the whole to be made from 4in concrete.

2 × 6 × 2 = 24 sq ft (6ft being the length of the deepest part of the pond)

2 × 3 × ½ = 3 sq ft (3ft being the length of the shallower part of the pond)

2 × 6 × 2 = 24 sq ft (this is the total for the sides; depth of shallow end = 1½ft + ½ft at shelf)

The total area is 51 sq ft

The base is 6 × 9 = 54 sq ft

The total area is 105 sq ft

A beautiful display of flowers surrounds this concrete pool.

The total volume is 105 × ⅓ = 35 cu ft

27 cu ft in a cu yd, therefore the amount of concrete required is 35 divided by 27 = approx. **1 ⅓ cu yds**

So, to build such a pond you would need 1 ⅓ cu yds of concrete.

In metric units Metric volumes are all expressed in cubic metres. Measure everything in metres and express the measurements as a whole number of metres plus the decimal part of the metre, for example, 10cm is 0.1m, and 60cm is 0.6m. Multiply the total area by 0.1m (10cm) to find the volume of cement required – the extra is necessary to

Japanese butterbur, Petasites japonicus.

provide a wall of 10cm thickness. W = width, D = depth, B = breadth.

Example To build a pond similar to the one described above, the calculations are as follows.

2 × 2 × 0.6 = 2.4 sq m

2 × 1 × 0.15 = 0.3 sq m

2 × 2 × 0.6 = 2.4 sq m

The total area of the sides of the pond = 5.1 sq m

The area of the base is 3 × 2 = 6 sq m

The total area is 6 = 5.1 = 11.1 sq m

The volume of concrete required to build such a pond to a thickness of 10cm is 11.1 × 0.1 = 1.11 cu m

Circular Ponds
The area of the side of a circular pond will be found by multiplying the radius by 2 then by π ($^{22}/_7$ or 3.142). The base is given by π times the radius squared.

On a pond of 6ft diameter, the boundary length will be 3 × 2 × $^{22}/_7$ = $^{132}/_7$ = 19 sq ft (approx.)

If the pond is uniformly 2ft deep then the area of the wall is 38 sq ft

The base is 3 × 3 × $^{22}/_7$ = $^{198}/_7$ = 28 sq ft (approx.)

The total area is 28 + 38 sq ft = 66 sq ft

The volume of concrete required for a thickness of 4in is $^{66}/_3$ = 22 cubic feet. (approx.)

If a shelf 6in deep is included, the total surface area to be covered with concrete is reduced by 1ft. This amount is insignificant and may be ignored for the purposes of calculation.

In metric units, a similar pond would be 2m in diameter, with a depth of 60cm.

The surface area of the side is 2 × 3.142 × 0.6 = 3.76 sq m

The surface area of the base is 3.142 × 1 = 3.142 sq m

The total surface area is 3.76 + 3.142 = 6.9 sq m

The total volume required for a thickness of 10cm = 0.69 cu m

Oval Ponds
The mathematics required to calculate the quantity of concrete for an oval pond are very complex. The best is to obtain an approximate value by assuming the minor and major axes are the sides of a rectangle, and calculate as for a rectangular pond. This will give you a greater volume of concrete than you actually need.

BUILDING THE CONCRETE POND STEP BY STEP

TOOLS AND MATERIALS

- ❀ Wheelbarrow
- ❀ Spade/shovel
- ❀ Trowel and float
- ❀ Spirit-level
- ❀ Wood for shuttering
- ❀ Hammer nails
- ❀ Chicken wire
- ❀ Cement and sand

Ponds should not be built during the worst parts of the winter and early spring, when drainage can present a problem; neither should concrete be laid during frosty weather when it will not set correctly, resulting in a lack of structural strength which can lead to cracking.

1. Decide the exact location.
2. Dig a hole 4in (10cm) deeper at all points and 8in (20cm) longer and wider than the intended dimensions of the pond to allow for the volume occupied by the cement. Make up the concrete to a mixture of five parts sand and gravel to two parts cement.

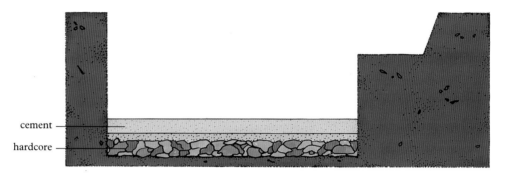

cement ——
hardcore ——

3. Lay the floor of the pond. Having levelled the site you may include hardcore, if available, and make up to 4in (10cm) with cement; or place a layer of about 2in (5cm) of concrete on the excavated surface, add chicken wire to provide extra strength and a further 2in (5cm) of cement mixture.
4. Using a builder's float, check the surface with a spirit-level to ensure that it is flat.
5. With small ponds, vertical sides are the only practical way of maximizing the deep water area. The

side of a pond is effectively a retaining wall and must possess sufficient thickness to provide adequate mechanical strength. To create the sides or retaining walls it is necessary to construct shuttering.

6. To make shuttering: create a four-sided bottomless and topless box of the size required, made with four corner pieces of 2 × 2in (5 × 5cm) wood, to which is nailed ½–1in (1–3cm) thick floor or weather boarding. Incorporate two cross members to give the structure additional strength.

7. Place the frame on the dried concrete base of the pond. Check that there is a gap of 4in (10cm) between the shuttering and the wall of soil. Place blocks or other heavy objects inside the frame to ensure that it cannot move.

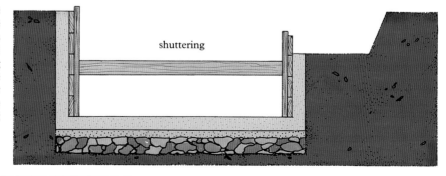

shuttering

BUILDING THE CONCRETE POND STEP-BY-STEP

shuttering for concrete-lined pools

8. Before applying the cement thoroughly soak the shuttering. When it dries, cement contracts and the amount of shrinkage will depend upon how wet the mixture was originally. If the boards are well soaked the mixture will be very wet in the region of the wood causing extra shrinkage and the shuttering will readily come away from the concrete wall. Reinforce the concrete by placing a piece of 1in (2.5cm) mesh chicken wire in the middle of the space to be filled with concrete. Pour in the concrete taking care that it is distributed either side of the chicken wire.
9. Allow the cement to dry out completely before removing the shuttering.

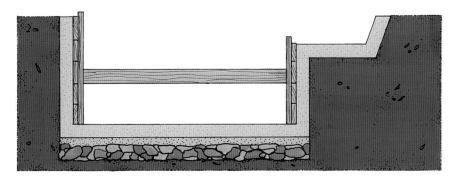

The ledges for marginals may extend around the whole pond but, from a design point, will usually be needed only at the side furthest from the usual observation point. Construct the shelf as for the base, omitting the hardcore but including chicken wire. The remaining vertical faces will require constructing with the aid of shuttering, as described for the main vertical area. Larger ponds can be constructed with a slope, which removes the necessity for shuttering. Construct a hollow dish shape, 3–4ft (1–1⅓m) at the centre, gradually sloping away to meet the natural level of the land.

SUMMARY

1. Excavate the site.
2. Check that all areas are level at the base.
3. Cover the base with a 4in (10cm) layer of concrete incorporating chicken wire to give the additional strength. Allow the concrete to set before proceeding.
4. Place shuttering up the sides of the pond as far as the ledge, leaving a 4in (10cm) gap in all directions. Place a piece of chicken wire down the gaps.
5. Force concrete between the shuttering and the wall, making sure that there are no gaps. Allow the concrete to set before proceeding.
6. Place a 4in (10cm) layer of concrete on the shelf, again incorporating the chicken wire. Allow the concrete to set before proceeding.
7. Place shuttering around the outer wall in the same manner as for the inner structure and fill with concrete.

Pond shapes in addition to the simple single geometrical design.

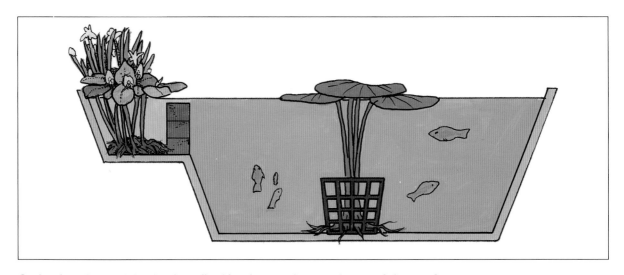

Section through a pond showing the walls with at least 15° batters to increase their strength. The marginals are planted in troughs created by a brickwork structure, whilst the water-lilies are planted in a purpose-built container.

Careful choice of shape is extremely important in terms of the design of the garden as a whole.

POND LINERS

Using pond liners represents the most versatile of the methods of pond construction, providing a barrier or membrane between the soil and the water. The shape of the pond is first excavated, then a layer of plastic sheeting is placed into the hole, which is filled with water. Providing that the plastic does not break, the pond will be a permanent structure. The success of the method depends not only on the method of construction but on the nature of the material from which the liner is made. All the different materials that are available are plastics made from products obtained mainly from crude petroleum. Several molecules of the starting material are joined together to form the plastic; the, individual properties of the plastics will depend upon that starting material, and may vary quite considerably in spite of the names appearing to be similar. Some plastics carry the prefix 'poly', denoting that several molecules are involved, whereas others do not, but the process of manufacture of all of them is similar.

The name 'plastic' means pliable and, although many of the petroleum-based materials are only mouldable at high temperatures, some do retain a degree of elasticity at ambient temperature. This is essential when the pond is being filled with water, to ensure that any slight stretching as a result of uneven water pressure does not permanently damage the membrane.

The main plastics used for pond liners are:

Butyl rubber This is the most widely used of the pond lining materials and may be safely recommended for use in all water garden constructions.
Polyvinylchloride (PVC) This is a plastic material that is used extensively in horticulture. The thicker sheets are a useful material for pond construction.
Plastolene This effectively overcomes the main problem associated with PVC sheeting (which is reduced mechanical strength), by reinforcing with a matrix of another plastic.

For a more accurate estimate, mark out a grid divided into 12in (30cm) squares, and draw the oval on the grid. Count the squares covered by the oval, and then add up the fractions of the squares that are not completely covered. This should give you a reasonably accurate estimate of the area involved. Multiply the area by 4in (⅓ft; 10cm) to give the volume of cement required in cubic feet.

The boundary of such a pond is best found by marking out the site and using a piece of string to define the circumference. The length of the string is multiplied by the depth and the thickness of the concrete to give the volume necessary for the pond wall. This volume, together with that of the base, is the total amount of concrete required.

Irregular-shaped Ponds
For irregular ponds, use the grid method described above for working out the area of an oval pond.

The Size of the Sheeting

You will need a piece of sheeting that covers the area of the pond, plus both the length and the

CONSTRUCTING THE LINED POND STEP-BY-STEP

TOOLS AND MATERIALS

- ❀ Wheelbarrow
- ❀ Spirit-level
- ❀ Sand
- ❀ Hose
- ❀ Spade/shovel
- ❀ Trowel
- ❀ Liner

1. Excavate the pond to the required size and shape, making sure that there are no sharp edges.
2. Smooth all surfaces and line with a 1in (2–3cm) layer of sand.

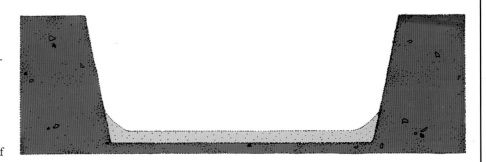

3. Lay the sheet over the hole, holding it in place with pieces of stone.
4. Place the outlet of the hose in the centre of the pond and allow it to fill with a controlled trickle.

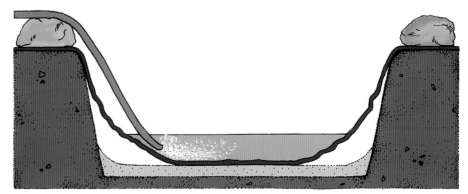

5. If necessary, release the stones to avoid stretching of the sheet.
6. When the pond is full, place paving stones around the outside.

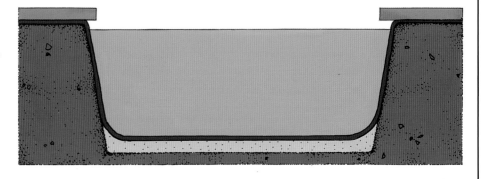

TIP

New materials are constantly appearing on the market and many are designed with repair in mind. Before buying any material for making a pond, ask about the availability of repair kits: you never know when they might be needed.

breadth increased by twice the depth, together with a further 3ft (1m) to provide an 18in (50cm) overlay around the pond.

For a rectangular pond 9ft (270cm) × 6ft (180cm) and 2ft (60cm) deep, the length required is:

9 + 2 + 2 + 1½ + 1½ = 16 ft, or

3 + 0.6 + 0.6 + 0.45 + 0.45 = 5.1m

The breadth required is:

6 + 2 + 2 +1½ + 1½ ＝ 13ft, or

2 + 0.6 + 0.6 + 0.45 + 0.45 = 4.1m

No reduction can be made at this stage for the shelf for marginals. The extra overlap should simply be cut away.

If you intend to include a bog garden in the scheme, add on the area in square feet that you wish to include, either to the length or the breadth, whichever is the most appropriate. For an irregular shaped pond the largest width and breadth must be taken, and the whole treated as though it were a rectangular pond, with the excess being trimmed away.

FIBREGLASS PONDS

Fibreglass is a material consisting of a plastic resin reinforced with strands of glass, which is readily moulded into a whole range of different shapes and sizes, including precast pond moulds. These pond moulds are sometimes shunned by garden purists as being restrictive in both shape and size, however, they are really a modern product designed for today's market, satisfying the needs of owners of smaller gardens. As such, they are the most suitable

Fibreglass pools are available in various shapes and sizes.

INSTALLING A FIBREGLASS POOL STEP-BY-STEP

1. With fibreglass pools most of the work has been done, and all that you need to do is to excavate a hole about ½in (1.5cm) wider than the mould at all points, and 2in (5cm) deeper so that the lip of the mould will lie below the ground level. Check for any stones or other debris that could puncture the shell or prevent it from lying flat. If the base of the hole is unfirm or full of flints, remove a further 4in (10cm) of soil and replace it with damp sand to form a smooth, level base.

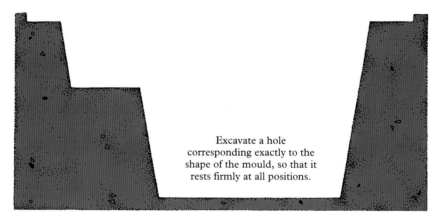

Excavate a hole corresponding exactly to the shape of the mould, so that it rests firmly at all positions.

2. Line the base with a 2in (5cm) layer of damp sand (an extra 2in (5cm) if you have already laid 4in (10cm) in step 1). Use the spirit-level to check that the base is quite level.

3. Lower the mould into place, and check again that it is level. If not, it will be necessary to remove the mould and rectify the problem before repeating the process.

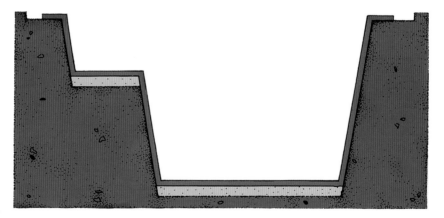

4. Pour dry sand down the gap between the mould and the walls of the hole so that all points of the mould's base rest on a firm foundation. Use the spirit-level at regular intervals to check that the mould has not moved. When all gaps have been filled, rest each end of a plank on the lips of the mould and place the spirit-level on top of it to check that it has remained precisely level.

5. When you are satisfied that the mould is firm and level, cover the lip of the mould with soil or rocks.

6. Place the hose in the centre of the mould and fill the pool by allowing water to trickle slowly into the shell. (This is important because if the pool is filled too quickly, the rush of water may cause the mould to shift slightly.) Use the spirit-level on the plank to check at regular intervals that the mould has remained firm and level.

choice for a variety of locations. Fibreglass liners do tend to be expensive compared with pond liners, and you must be careful when placing them into position not to damage them. Many fibreglass liners are too shallow, so ensure that the one you buy has a large enough area and a depth of 2ft (60cm), to enable you to keep fish and to allow you some choice with your water-lilies.

Fibreglass moulds are often carelessly sited, with the result that the plastic material protrudes on to the landscape. Unless the container is invisible it will spoil the view, but this is avoidable. Some plastic liners are sold with an edge that is moulded to appear like rocks. When buying such products you should seek out the very best, otherwise the effect will not be attractive.

THE SINK POND

Sink gardens, in which an old sink or receptacle of similar size is planted with alpines, cacti or other suitable subjects, and used as an adjunct to the main garden, are a well-established principle. Less familiar are sink ponds. These are miniature pools which are placed in a garden at a suitable position, and fulfil part of the role of the pond, but are insignificant in landscaping terms. No garden is so small that it cannot accommodate a sink pond. In the minutest townscape, the smallest fibreglass liner may be purchased and employed in a miniature layout in a similar way to a true pond in a larger area. However, there is one important difference between this and a true water garden – because of

---

CONSTRUCTING A SINK POND STEP-BY-STEP

1. Acquire an old sink – depth is more important than surface area, and you should look out for a vessel at least 9in (22.5cm) deep. Block the drainage hole.
2. If you intend to site the vessel above ground level, remove the glaze from the sink and create a natural-looking finish by roughly covering with a mixture of two parts cement, one part peat, and four parts sand. This will soon age and give an appearance similar to that of natural rock.
3. Fill the miniature pool with water, and plant waterweed to ensure an adequate supply of oxygen.

A waterproof barrel makes an attractive miniature pond for the patio.

the reduced depth and mass of water, freezing solid is a very real possibility and any fish will need to be wintered in an aquarium. This should not cause any disturbance to their development as they can be transferred to an aquarium of a similar size.

You are not restricted here just to sinks, and use can be made of any suitable vessel. Care should be taken to ensure that the vessel is of suitable strength; many plastics will, if exposed to the weather, begin a gradual disintegration accelerated by the frost. These may not remain outside in the winter, and it will be necessary to store them in a frost-free place in order to protect the material from which they are made. Special containers may be purchased which can be sited outside during the winter.

With the sink or miniature pond you will not be able to achieve as much as with a complete pond, but one ideal use is for raising the dwarf water-lily. The vessel functions as a flower pot, with water replacing and taking on the role of the majority of the soil. This is particularly applicable to the patio layout, where special importance is attached to container gardening.

If it is situated in a part of the garden where there is little disturbance, even such a small expanse of water will feature as a natural habitat, and many creatures may be attracted to it. Frogs and newts are no strangers to such sites, and will amply repay you by consuming pests.

Even the small patio can usually accommodate a sink pond, in this case below ground.

BOG GARDENS

Artificial bog gardens can be made on a smaller
scale, the same way as the large pond is constructed.

A clay trough as a moisture-
retaining liner filled with a rich
soil-peat mixture.

A heavy-gauge plastic sheet
with drainage holes, which is
filled with growing mix.

A glass-fibre or plastic water
cistern with drainage holes.

RAISED PONDS

In spite of the problems associated with very cold spells, raised ponds fit ideally into a terrace landscaping scheme, especially one involving retaining walls and hanging gardens growing in the spaces between the bricks. They are also ideal for the handicapped for whom bending down may present a problem. With a raised pond there is an opportunity to feed and study the fish at your leisure and enjoy the pleasures of gardening without being restricted by disabilities. Raised ponds can be expensive to build. Water exerts a pressure in all directions, so a fairly strong wall is needed to retain this. To contribute to the strength of the structure it will be best to build a concrete pond, for which a double-leaf wall should be built. The problem here is to produce a structure with a sufficiently high tensile strength, and to guarantee success professional help should be sought.

A plastic or even a fibreglass liner may be used, providing there is a strong retaining wall, built with a 15° batter.

An alternative approach to a step-wise garden is to

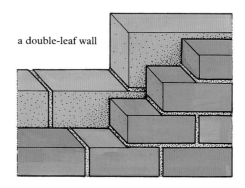

a double-leaf wall

excavate out the soil 2ft (60cm) below the level of the terrain, and build the retaining wall for the whole of the terrace from this depth. Part or all of the lower level of the terrace will now be a water garden. Such an approach provides one of the most efficient uses of a sloping site.

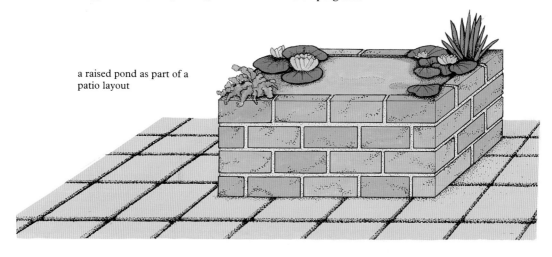

a raised pond as part of a patio layout

CHAPTER 3

Establishing the Pond

THE BALANCE OF NATURE

However carefully we seek to control the pond environment by providing lilies and other plants together with fish that have been bred primarily to appeal to our aesthetic sense, rather than to survive, the pond will always remain a natural world, under the control of natural, not man-made, forces. If there is not enough food in the water, fish will die; conversely if there are too many minerals in the water, organisms will colonize it and exploit the food supply, producing green filamentous algae or single cellular micro-organisms which will result in a thick cloudy soup-like water. To be a successful pond keeper it is necessary to harness the natural forces to work for you and to produce the effects that you seek; left unmanaged nature will create a wilderness of your pond.

An attractive well-balanced pond.

Oxygen

The fact that fish live in water does not mean that they do not require oxygen, only that the process by which they extract it from their environment is different to that used by terrestrial creatures.

Air dissolves in water, thus providing the oxygen supply for all aquatic creatures that depend upon it. Two factors influence the quantity of oxygen that can enter the water from the air: the water's surface area and the water's temperature. The larger the surface area and the lower the temperature of the water, the greater the amount of air that can be dissolved. These are important facts for the pond keeper to bear in mind when designing and managing the water garden because, although the oxygen in the air is more soluble than the nitrogen – and will therefore enter the water in greater quantity than nitrogen – oxygen dissolves quite slowly. Anything that the gardener can do to maximize the amount of oxygen in the water, and the rate at which it enters it, is to the benefit of pond creatures.

It is possible to increase the surface area of the water without actually enlarging the pond by adding a fountain or waterfall: by breaking water into droplets or creating a falling curtain, a greater surface area is produced which, albeit only temporary, is sufficient to increase the quantity of air that can be dissolved. This secondary role of water is not always appreciated; the pump need not be kept running at all times, but only on warm days.

Another very important source of oxygen is water weed; those plants that grow beneath the surface of the water. They liberate oxygen by photosynthesis, in which they break down the carbon dioxide liberated by the fish.

The amount of oxygen available in the water is a critical factor in determining the number of fish that a pond can sustain. When calculating this, it should be borne in mind that fish are not the only ones requiring oxygen, so the amount of oxygen available to them will be influenced by the numbers of other creatures sharing their environment, such as water snails. Having said this, fish will account for most of the oxygen used, since water snails and other similar creatures are far less active and their requirements therefore smaller, which means that unless

A flourishing well-oxygenated larger pond with a statuette to add a classical touch.

WAYS TO MAXIMIZE AVAILABLE OXYGEN

1. Design a pool with the greatest possible surface area.
2. Include a fountain or waterfall in the design to augment the supply during warm weather.
3. Plant sufficient water weed to generate oxygen in the water itself.

THE BALANCE OF OXYGEN

OXYGEN ENTERS THE WATER:

❋ By dissolving at the surface
❋ By aeration
❋ By release from water weed and other plants through photosynthesis

OXYGEN IS TAKEN FROM THE WATER:

❋ By the respiration of fish
❋ By the microbes of decay
❋ By being released to the atmosphere on a warm day when the gas is no longer soluble.

they are present in very large numbers they will not unduly affect the sustainable fish population. It must also be remembered that oxygen demand varies with the time of year: during the winter, when fish are relatively inactive, they require far less oxygen than they do when they are very active; activity peaks during the breeding season, reproduction demanding high energy.

The pond's oxygen supply can be depleted by decaying animal and plant tissue. Decay is brought about by microbes which require oxygen to liberate the energy necessary for their life processes. Although the microbes are tiny and invisible to the naked eye individually, the countless millions that exist together will soon deplete a pond of oxygen. A single dead bird or fish could be sufficient to stop an average-size pond from supporting life, as could an accumulation of leaves and other garden detritus over the autumn and winter months.

Oxygen levels decrease with depth, so life that exists in the lower reaches of the pond has evolved to do without free oxygen, instead taking up the oxygen chemically bound within the energy-giving materials themselves. This way of life without air is termed 'anaerobic respiration'. The microbes which cause decay at the bottom of the pool live anaerobically and, for this reason, the loam or well-rotted manure in which water-lilies are planted will not lead to a critical reduction in the oxygen level. However the amount of such humus material must be carefully controlled, as it will release compounds into the water which will encourage the growth of water-fouling microbes.

Nutrients

Water-lilies and other pond plants require the correct amount of minerals: nitrogen, phosphates and potassium, as well as trace elements. As with oxygen there is a critical balance: insufficient nutrients will retard growth, while too much will lead to the rapid growth of microbes causing the pond to become cloudy. *The correct level of nutrients is the single most important factor in obtaining clear pond water.*

The roots of bottom-growing plants such as lilies do not take up minerals as do their terrestrial counterparts. Their role is purely one of anchorage. The nutrients are taken in by the modified stems which have an enlarged surface area. The roots of floating plants have no anchorage function, their role is

Zebra rush, Scirpus tabernaemontani 'Zebrinus'.

**PLANTS AND FISH PER
100 sq ft (10m²)**

❀ Three water-lilies.
❀ Fifteen marginal units (Reed mace and Arrow-head will count as three units each, all others as one).
❀ Fish, stock at the density of 1in (2.5cm) of fish per 1 gallon (4.5 litres) (Allowance must be made for fish growth. With fish it is safer to understock than to overstock.)

---

simply to gulp in dissolved minerals. The aim of the pond is to sustain the maximum amount of plant life consistent with clear water, which is far more and of greater variety than would be found in any natural habitat. To achieve any degree of success a source of nutrients is essential.

One well-established method consists of providing a small quantity of well-rotted cow manure every three or four years. This corresponds to the average length of time that is required to thin out water-lilies. Without realizing it, gardeners who for years raised their lilies and replanted them in well-rotted manure were not only controlling the growth of the plants but providing the pond with a constant source of naturally controlled discharging minerals. Only now is science beginning to understand and explain what has been learned by trial and error over many years. With manure becoming increasingly difficult to obtain, chemical substitutes have been developed. By choosing salts of the correct solubility it is possible to release measured doses over a period, and this has lead to pelleted forms of fertilizers for ponds. These are extremely useful but it is important that you know the volume of water and the correct amount to add. Never add general purpose or other fertilizer designed for garden use to ponds! They may be toxic to fish and the sudden abundance of nutrients will almost certainly lead to cloudy water.

Light

Light is the third factor in getting the balance of the pond correct. Provided underwater oxygenators, such as water weed, get sufficient light, they will compete with the microbes responsible for causing cloudy water and stop their development. However, an excess of light can lead to problems and the aim should be for half of the area of the pond to be covered with the floating leaves of water-lilies.

THE WATER

Tap water may contain a quantity of chlorine as well as various dissolved mineral salts, particularly calcium and magnesium. However, the initial filling of your pond may be with tap water, as the water weed will produce oxygen which will quickly replace the chlorine. If the system is a allowed a week to a fortnight to settle down, there is very little danger of the gas being present in any significant amount. The mineral salts may be ignored. Once a pond has been filled, the water is under threat from two natural forces: first, evaporation will reduce the volume to an appreciable extent during the summer months, and then there is the problem of rising toxicity. No matter how careful you are, you will not succeed in stopping all of the detritus of the garden from entering the pond. This, together with any waste products that the wildlife builds up, will result in the water becoming progressively less and less suitable for supporting the types of life that we require.

The most effective method of maintaining the sweetness of the water is to have a hose pipe feeding into the pond from the gutters of the house. This will supply water to the pond whenever there is any rainfall, maintaining the level during the summer months without contributing any potentially harmful gases to the system or building up the dissolved solids in the water. Any excess water will run off into the surrounding garden area, and this is ideal if you have included a bog garden in your design. During the winter months the water will enter the pond and an exchange will take place, resulting in a continual replacement of water in the critical top third of the pond. Where it is not considered practical to lead the water straight from the roof to the pond, the rainfall should be collected from the gutter and into a water butt. The pond level can be periodically topped up with this water during the summer. The butt should be allowed to discharge until it is empty during late October and early April, thus ensuring an intermittent replacement of the water.

The amount of water you that will require will depend upon the size of the pond; if it is only small, you will not need the drainage from the whole of the roof. To avoid a greater discharge than the water garden needs, water falling on small areas, such as a shed or a greenhouse, both of which can be fitted with gutters, should be considered. If tap water is the only practical possibility, top up during the summer and treat during autumn and spring as described for rainwater. Check first with the water authority if you do not have a licence for a hose pipe. With a relatively large bog garden a supplementary water supply from the tap will be essential during the summer months, and if you are using tap water there is no reason why you should not route this through the pond itself.

A new pond inevitably takes some time to reach its equilibrium. Once the pond has been filled with water, you should immediately plant the water weeds and water-lilies. At this stage there will be an excess of nutrients and oxygen, and this will inevitably lead to the growth of algae which will cloud the water. Allow the system about a week to settle down before adding the fish and the water snails. The excess of micro-organisms will be consumed by pond inhabitants, which are soon transported to any new source of water, and in a very short time the water will gradually turn crystal clear. The length of time taken for this will depend upon how quickly the balance of nature can be reached. All changes, such as the replacement of the soil around the lilies or a massive exchange of water in the spring or autumn (where a continual method of replenishing the supply is not used) can lead to a clouding of the water, but the equilibrium

The goodness of this water is illustrated by the healthy fish and plants.

STAGNANT WATER

Any pond will be incapable of supporting life if the water becomes stagnant. Stagnant water results from large quantities of vegetable matter entering the pond. As well as the system becoming deficient in oxygen, the water will gradually dissolve out increasing amounts of the acid tannin, rendering the medium unsuitable for any forms of life. The usual sign is when the water acquires a brown coloration from the leaves. Natural ponds which are particularly liable to become stagnant may additionally acquire a brown coloration if there is any ironstone in the district, as the acid water begins to dissolve the iron out. A third source of brown coloration is certain micro-organisms which contain a pigment of that colour. Another feature which accompanies stagnation is a rainbow seen on the top of pond water, due to a very thin film of oil on the surface. The problems of stagnation will be avoided if the water maintenance programme outlined above is followed.

CAUTION

Do not plant too many water-lilies: if all light is excluded the water weed will not be able to generate the necessary oxygen to sustain life.

---

will soon be re-established and the water will become clear again. This clouding should never be used as an excuse for not adopting the routine methods of pond maintenance which are essential if the best results are to be achieved.

WATER CLARITY

When first established, or following the annual overhaul, the pond's water will be cloudy. This will settle as the humus particles responsible for the lack of clarity gradually sink. Until the lilies have established their growth they also may cause some discoloration of the water owing to the presence of microbes, which they encourage. However, this, too, should soon clear. Algae will also reduce clarity. It is made up of many minute plants, and can be divided into two main types. The first, filamentous algae, consists of individual cells grouped together to form long strands termed blanket weed. This should be removed by twirling it round a stick;

it can then be safely transferred to the compost heap. The second type of algae consists of cells which float in groups on the surface, producing a scum. Periodic flooding with rainwater will remove this problem or it may be scooped from the water using a bucket, although it will be necessary to replace this water with fresh. Often ponds appear green. This is created by millions of single-cell floating plants, which develop either because there is insufficient water weed to soak up the excess minerals, or because there is too much light, which happens when there is insufficient water-lily cover. Cure the problem planting weeds and lilies as necessary.

In a well-established pond with sufficient water weed (it is difficult to have too much), there will seldom be a problem: in the early spring, when the water is beginning to warm up and plants are springing back into life weed will compete for the light, thereby maintaining clear water until high summer, by which time water-lily leaves will have covered part of the pool and eliminated the light.

SUMMARY OF FACTORS AFFECTING WATER CLARITY

❀ Oxygen
❀ Nutrients
❀ Light
❀ Fish and other life

All these factors must be in balance to ensure a safe environment.

CHAPTER 4

Pond Plants

WATER-LILIES

Water-lilies are by far the most important of the water garden plants, and it is virtually impossible to conceive a pond layout which does not contain at least one type. There are forty to fifty natural species of water-lily throughout the world, and some are tropical, requiring temperatures above those encountered in the average water garden. These need ponds which are artificially heated, or they may be grown in a conservatory or even the house as an aquarium subject. Other species, however, are hardy and can withstand the British climate – one species is even native to Britain. Water-lilies may be found in all of the primary colours, including light blue, and the anthers are often a different colour from the petals, which may vary quite considerably in number. All water-lilies contain four sepals. Some are richly perfumed. The flowers seem to appear as if by magic from the water, and are brilliantly coloured, so it is not surprising that water-lilies feature in the folklore of many peoples.

The water-lily is probably the most popular of all aquatic subjects.

PLANTING WATER-LILIES STEP-BY-STEP

1. Fill a plastic basket with compost.

2. Plant the root and cover the compost with gravel.

3. Submerge the basket to the depth recommended for the variety you are planting.

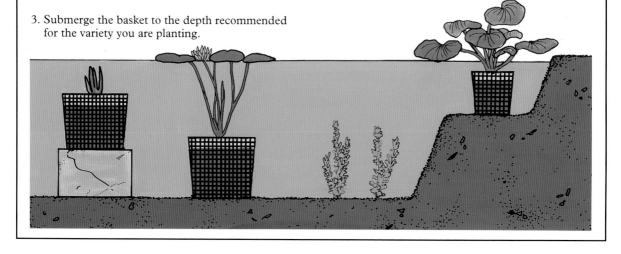

DEPTH OF WATER

VARIETY	COLOUR	(in/cm)	REMARKS
'Albida'	White	18–36/45–90	Latour-Marliac hybrid
'Carnea'	Pink to white	18–36/45–90	Latour-Marliac hybrid
'Chromatella'	Yellow	18–36/45–90	Strong-growing, long-flowering Latour-Marliac hybrid
'Escarboucle'	Red	18–24/45–60	One of the most popular of all reds
'Firecrest'	Pale to deep pink	18–24/45–60	Medium-sized flowers
'Frobobelii'	Red	12–24/30–60	A very prolific plant
'Fulgens'	Pinkish red	12–24/30–60	Laydeker hybrid
'Gladstonia'	White	60–72/150–180	The largest of all water-lilies
'Helvola'	White	9–12/20–30	The smallest of the water-lilies
'James Brydon'	Pink to rose	12–30/30–75	A very popular hybrid
'Paul Hariot'	Red to pink	12–18/30–45	Vigorous hybrid
'Purpurata'	Pink to red	12–24/30–60	Laydeker hybrid
'Rosea'	Pink to white	18–24/45–60	Latour-Marliac hybrid
'Sunrise'	Yellow to golden	12–18/30–45	Large-flowered cultivar

THE SPECIES OF WATER-LILIES

All water-lilies take the genus name *Nymphaea* ('water nymph') and then a second (species) name which usually describes some particular characteristic of the individual species. Sometimes species produce sports or varieties distinct from the usual form, and these are given a third name denoting that variety.

Both species and hybrids can be further sub-divided into hardy and tender. The tender species require varying degrees of artificial heat and are only suitable for ponds which will have a heating system of growing in a conservatory or even as an aquarium 'pot plant', so they need not be considered further. Hybridizing records are not complete, so it is not always possible to state with any degree of certainty whether a particular form is a naturally-occurring species or a man-made variety. Some species occurring in the wild may be the result of natural hybridization.

N. alba This is the white water-lily, and the only species native to Britain. It is capable of prospering at a depth of 2–4ft (60–120cm).

N. odorata The fragrant water-lily, and one of the most important of all varieties in the hybridization programme. The original white form comes from the U.S.A. Popular varieties include *N. odorata* 'Sulphurea' (a bright, pale yellow variety), and a larger form, *N. odorata* 'Sulphurea Grandiflora' which is extremely fragrant – with flowers of 6in (15cm) or more in diameter, it is too large for the smaller ponds. Generally, water-lilies are not strongly fragrant, but either of these will help to attract a large range of insects to the pond.

N. candida This is a natural white, which is smaller than *N. alba*.

N. fennica This is a small white form which may have been involved in the production of some of the miniatures.

N. pygmaea alba The white miniature water-lily. It is probably not a pure species, and may contain either *N. candida* or *N. tetragona* (or both) in its make-up.

N. pygmaea alba 'Helvola' This is the smallest of all water-lilies, and is a subject especially suited to miniature pond layouts, since it requires a water depth of only 12in (30cm). The flowers are a pale yellow or cream shade.

N. tetragona A natural miniature with small white flowers.

N. tuberosa A large water-lily of American origin, which requires quite a deep pond.

Underwater baskets can be useful for planting water-lilies.

THE HYBRID WATER-LILIES

Often the exact origin of a lily is not known; like roses, they bear just a single name, such as 'Escarboucle' or 'James Brydon', and this will be prefaced by the family name to give 'Nymphaea Escarboucle'. Where the name of the original hybridist is known this is usually commemorated, to give, for example, *Nymphaea × laydekeri* or *Nymphaea × marliacea* (referring to the two Frenchmen, M Laydeker and M Latour-Marliac, pioneers in water-lily cultivar production). This is followed by the name of the variety.

As with all plants, the selective hybrids have larger flowers, better form and perfume, brighter colours, and perhaps a longer flowering season than the species. Virtually everyone will find that the hybrids offer better choice and, with the exception of some of the varieties, it is highly unlikely that anyone other than the hybridist will wish to cultivate the species type.

The table opposite shows some of the most popular of the many hardy hybrids available.

Growing Water-lilies

Water-lilies require a rich compost, of five parts of good quality loam and one part of well-rotted manure. The mixture may either be deposited at the bottom of the pond and the lilies allowed to root freely, or it may be placed in a container which is little more than a lattice effect allowing the water to circulate. Restricting the roots in a container reduces the vigour of the growth, resulting in smaller plants and reduced pond cover. This is not necessarily a disadvantage, as it does allow you to grow some of the more vigorous species in smaller ponds. One simple method of planting is to place the water-lily root, together with a small amount of compost, in a stocking and place this in the pond.

Even the small amounts of nutrient from this can lead to an excess of minerals, leading in turn to the growth of large amounts of algae, but the rapid growth of the lilies will soon take over and provide the necessary surface cover to produce clear water.

Water-lilies grow quickly, and they will cover the surface of the pond in three to five years, when they must be thinned out. In May, before there is much growth, remove the old root, and with a sharp knife cut it until you have pieces with three strong eyes (weaker eyes may be removed). Replant in fresh compost. Do not replant unless there has been overcrowding – size rather than time must be the deciding factor, as some species can prosper for many seasons without totally dominating. The exact frequency of replanting varies with different types.

Hardy water-lilies (Nymphaea) *in variety (below).*

Pure white is as useful a colour in water gardens as in its terrestrial equivalent (opposite).

Varieties to Choose From

Unlike most other garden subjects, you will find that you have room for very few water-lilies – you will probably only be able to have one or two in the size of pond that is most suited to the smaller urban and estate gardens. It is essential that you make the correct choice in the first place, to avoid the expensive need to replace the flowers if you are not content with the variety. You must carefully consider the choice of colours (and there is a large range), because water-lilies are often in very bright shades and must therefore be thought of in terms of their total contribution to the garden. They also vary quite considerably in terms of their coverage and the depth of water that they require. Flower forms differ very much from the open, almost flat, star-shaped varieties, where the sharp petals radiate from the centre to the points of the compass, through the dahlia types (there is even one 'water-lily' classification for certain exhibition dahlias), to the tight global-shaped doubles such as 'James Brydon', which imitate the peony.

The leaves which appear fresh each spring also vary from pale green through to dark green shot with red. Some varieties have buds of one colour, which open and then gradually change colour. Even the opening of the blooms creates variety, with the water-lily's tendency to open and close with the sun – some types are only open when the sun is at its very brightest, just before and after noon.

Water-lilies are classified by being divided into two groups – the species (those forms which occur naturally in the wild), and the hybrids (the results of crossing species or other hybrids together). Depending upon the variety, water-lilies require different growing depths and, whilst there is often a wide range of water levels which they can tolerate, you should not grow them in the wrong depth of water. For this reason, where you wish to grow a variety you must consider this before designing your pond to ensure that you have suitable conditions. The varying depth can be incorporated to include more than one variety. Pots may be placed on supports to artificially create shallower water conditions, if these are required. Because of the importance of the water-lily, especially in formal layouts, the pond should be thought of as the housing for the lily, rather than the lily as a plant to place in the pond.

BOG PLANTS

Bog plants range from those that grow in permanently wet soil, but not submerged (as in the case of the true marginals), to those that require permanently damp soil. Many plants are not too exacting in their requirements. Some marginals, such as the irises, will survive only in permanently damp soil, whilst others, such as *Trollius* and some of the primulas will grow in normal beds provided that they are never allowed to dry out. From this very wide range of plants we can choose those best suited to growing beside the pond.

Aconitum (Aconitum), Monk's Hood or Wolf's-bane

A great favourite in the cottage garden, this plant was originally used by the ancient Britons who dipped their spears into an extract of the roots, which contained sufficient poison to kill even the largest wolves, hence the popular name.

However, great care must be taken with the plant as all parts are extremely poisonous, especially the bright red berries which appear after the flowers. *A. napellus,* the European aconitum has a deep blue hood and there are several other varieties in cultivation. Aconitums are planted in the autumn or early spring and flower during mid- and late summer, with the berries following about a month later.

Astilbe (Spiraea)

These beautiful plants have feathery foliage and spikes carrying pink, white or red flowers made up of a collection of individual florets. A must for any bog garden – they can be raised from seed in the spring.

Euphorbia palustris

Like all the euphorbias or spurges, this has an almost succulent growth.

Ferns

Ferns constitute one of the oldest and most widespread groups of plant on earth. Very primitive,

*Flea bane (*Pulicaria dysenterica*).*

Dryopteris cristata Known as Buckler's fern it will reach a height and spread of 2ft (60cm). Curled, light brown stalks gradually unwind to reveal a thick central stem. Several stems in pairs emerge on opposite sides of the main stem, and it is these leaf-like structures which carry the spores. Tolerant of the moistest conditions (but not a marginal) it is hardy throughout moderate climates.
Phyllitis scolopendrium Hart's-tongue fern has a height and spread of 2ft (60cm). It has shiny mid-green strap-like fronds, which are undivided and rising from a crown. A fern of chalky areas, crushed chalk or oyster shell should be added to the leaf-mould compost of the soil in which it is planted. Totally hardy.
Polystichum aculeatum Consists of stalks which carry oppositely sited, deep-green, shiny fronds. A particularly beautiful fern, highly recommended. Totally hardy and tolerant of very wet conditions.

Gunnera manicata

This can be grown only in the larger water gardens where it is a must. It is a native of Brazil but is hardy in most temperate regions, including Britain, surviving even the severest winters. Straw, or the dead growth of the previous season, should be used to cover the crowns during the winter to provide the necessary protection. The gunnera has one of the largest florescences of any plant, and itself looks like a giant rhubarb.

Hosta (Plantain Lily)

A family of perennials grown almost exclusively for the colouring of the leaves, which are borne from mid-spring through to mid-autumn, although they do carry a stalk of lilac-coloured flowers in early summer. The leaves vary from dark to light brown with white and yellow marbling as variations.

Lobelia cardinalis (Cardinal Flower)

A useful, late season plant, its bright foliage tinted red which complements the spike of red flowers that appears in late summer. It sustains interest in the water garden until the end of the season. Sow seeds of the perennial in gentle heat during the

they do not produce flowers or seeds; reproduction is by spores (*see* Propagating Ferns, Chapter 9). The majority of ferns require damp, semi-shaded positions. Whilst many are frost-hardy, they tend to suffer from burning if planted in exposed or windswept areas, so they should always be grown in a sheltered position. More tender species can be planted out in flower pots for overwintering in the greenhouse, but there is such a wide and interesting range of hardy forms that this should not be necessary. Ferns should always be planted in a leaf-mould-based compost. Amongst the hardy forms suitable for growing beside ponds are:
Adiantum capillus veneris This fern has very thin stalks with several three-lobed fronds. Hardy only in fairly mild climates.

Hostas with their variegated leaves are an important component in the bog garden from late spring to mid-autumn.

spring, overwinter the first year in the cold greenhouse, and plant out into permanent position the following spring.

Lysichiton (syn *Lysichitum*) *americanum*

An arum-like plant which grows successfully in humus-rich, moist ground. Requiring far wetter conditions than most bog plants, it needs permanently wet soil. The species most frequently cultivated is the Skunk Cabbage, a giant member of the Araceae family.

Mimulus (Monkey-flower)

One of the few genera that is at home in both alpine and wetland conditions. Flowers are red and yellow, self-coloured or variegated, single or double,

depending upon which of the several species or cultivars you choose. This is a late-summer flowering plant, a rarity amongst bog garden plants which usually bloom during the spring.

Primula

The *Primula* family is very large, with groups ranging from alpines that require open, well-drained soil to the bog or waterside species. There is a range of colours in the red to yellow region of the spectrum as well as some blues. The group tends to flower in the late spring and early summer. The genus includes: *P. denticulata*, which has an almost globular head made up of several flowers in the red – purple range; *P. florindae*, an open type primula that is reminiscent of a cowslip and prospers in the water garden, growing to a height of 3ft (1m); *P. japonica*, the Japanese primula, which is another very vigorous species and can reach a height of 2ft

Mimulus, or the monkey flower, can add colour to your display. It is eminently suitable for poolside planting.

(60cm); and *P. pulverlum*, which is late-flowering. There are several other species of primula which flower in damp conditions but it is not easy to categorize them simply as wet or dry land plants.

Grunnera manicata growing with blue hostas and feathery ferns.

PRIMULAS SUITABLE FOR GROWING IN WET LOCATIONS

SPECIES	DESCRIPTION	FLOWERS
P. bulleyana	2ft (60cm), orange yellow flowers	Early summer
P. burmanica	2ft (60cm), red flowers	Early summer
#+*P. dentulata*	1ft (30cm), purple spherical flowers	Early summer
+*P. florindae*	2½ft (75cm), primrose yellow flowers	Early summer
#+*P. japonica*	1½–2ft (45–60cm), red flowers	Late spring
# *P. pulverulenta*	2ft (60cm), white to red flowers	Early summer
#+*P. vulgaris*	6in (15cm), various cultivars in red, yellow and purple	Spring

+ May be propagated by crown division after flowering.
# Many common garden raised cultivars in cultivation which may not germinate true from seed.

RAISING PRIMULAS STEP-BY-STEP

1. Seeds should be sown in early spring in a pan of sterilized, peat-based compost, the whole placed in a polythene bag to maintain humid conditions, and kept in gentle heat until they have germinated.
2. When large enough to handle, the seedlings should be pricked out individually into 3in (7.5cm) pots and kept in a cold greenhouse or frame. Harden off by placing the pots outside during the daytime and bringing them indoors at night.
3. Throughout the summer, the seedlings should be kept in slight shade with the compost permanently damp. If the compost is allowed to dry out at any stage, the plants will die. The plants will be ready for setting out the following spring.
4. Work some well-rotted manure or compost into the site before planting.
5. After flowering, remove the dead heads and stalks and propagate by lifting and dividing those species recommended above.
6. Where seed is to be collected, the dead flower heads must be allowed to remain, the seed heads placed in bags when they are brown, and shaken to remove the seeds, which should then be stored in a cool dry place until the following spring.

Note: It is often the case that only species of wild forms germinate true from seeds; many of the more spectacular cultivars produce unpredictable offspring or offspring that have reverted to the wild form.

Primula pulverulenta *in a bog garden.*

Rheum palmatum

This member of the rhubarb family which grows to 6–10ft (2–3m) with a similar spread is grown for its large feathery leaves. The blooms, which are carried on a tall stalk, consist of many small, individual, unspectacular blooms that should be removed as soon as flowering is complete. Suitable only for the largest gardens.

Trollius

This genus is a member of the Ranunculaceae or buttercup family. Some of the *Trollius* hybrids display globe-shaped flowers characteristic of the family; others, such as *T. pumulus*, have a flatter, more open flower. The plants may be placed in moist ground during autumn and will flower throughout the following summer. Dead heading will prolong the flowering period with some types. Seeds, which should be sown during the early spring and raised as described for *Primulas*, are slow germinating.

Zantedeschia aethiopica

Another of the water plants with arum-type florescence. In the spring, it has a white flower with a yellow centre. The variety 'Crowborough' is the one most frequently grown.

The Trollius *or globe flower provides yellow buttercup-like flowers in the bog garden throughout May and June.*

DRY BORDERS

A bog garden is by no means essential to the success of the pond, although it is an extremely useful option, in that it offers the opportunity to grow some very interesting plants which might otherwise be overlooked in garden planning. However, there are other ways of dealing with the land around the pool. One of the most popular of the dry borders is a variation on the alpine theme. With geometrically shaped pools, bright bedding plants may be used as a contrast to the subdued shades of water and the building materials. You should avoid any plants which grow over 1ft (30cm), as they will tend to obliterate the low-growing water-lilies.

DRY BORDER SUBJECTS

SPRING

Ideal subjects include *Compositae* (daisies), *Iris reticulata*, *Narcissii* (various), pansies (winter), *Polyanthus*, snowdrops and tulips (kaufmaniana).

SUMMER

Include antirrhinums, begonias (both tuberous and fibrous-rooted), lobelia, pansies (summer), *Salvia*, stocks, and *Tagetes*.

A pool with a rockery or alpine garden.

Purple loosestrife (Lythrum salicaria).

Two plantings, in spring and autumn, will be necessary to ensure that interest is maintained for as long as possible in any year. But even then, there exists a period from mid-autumn to early spring when, unless you are careful, there will be only minimal interest in the ponds, and its surroundings and the garden as a whole will look very jaded. In creating a garden for all seasons, water and the surrounding stone will blend well with heather and dwarf conifers. Depending upon the variety, heather will flower from early autumn through to late spring in a range of whites, purples and reds. Dwarf conifers create year-long interest through their cones, which exhibit the most diverse variety of shapes and tones; new growth will range from a buff shade through to deep red. Foliage colour varies from the green of *Picea* to the blue of *Juniperus*, with all their mutations in whites, yellows and golds. However, the most interesting feature is that

of form. Dwarf conifers grow in a variety of shapes, which may be based on a column, a cone or a horizontal spread, providing weed-choking ground cover. Careful selection of the various shapes will create a backcloth with perfect balance that will set the pool off and retain its shape (aided if necessary by some judicious pruning) throughout the changing of the seasons.

In any garden during the dark days of late autumn and winter, apart from a few straggling species of winter cherry, Chinese witch hazel and *Viburnum*, there is little to create interest other than the heathers and conifers. These can be used as part of a raised mound in conjunction with a small quantity of stone. The stone is present purely for visual effect, and the structure should not be confused with a rockery where more stone is used with an important ecological contribution to make. Such a feature is not intended to produce colour in

South African Lily, Zantedeschia aethiopica.

portion – too large a structure will not be in keeping with the smaller pool most suited to the urban garden. Aim to raise the bed no more than 3ft (1m), and at the centre of the mound place brick rubble and other drainage materials before covering with top soil. This should be of good quality loam, and part of the soil excavated for the pond itself may be used. Add a handful of bone-meal per surface square yard of the mound, to provide the slow-release nutrients that are so important with trees and shrubs. Do not add any general fertilizer as this will result in fast, soft growth, which will be incapable of withstanding the winter.

Your dry border can be the ideal setting for a watercourse. Again, this illustrates the importance of considering all the design aspects of water gardening together.

MARGINALS

These are plants which prefer to grow with their roots permanently under between 2 and 6in (5–15cm) of water. Despite this fact, they are land plants, and they will have a rapidly spreading rootstock. Left unchecked, the stronger varieties will rapidly take over. You could simply cover the bottom of the pond with rich compost and plant, but the result will be the same as in a garden where the subject such as couch grass has been allowed to

the manner of a summer bedding surround, none the less you may need to add to it to maintain interest during bright days of spring and summer. Plant a few very bright subjects, such as snowdrops, miniature narcissi and gentians, being careful not to over-plant.

With a dry border such as this drainage is essential, but it is important to keep everything in pro-

Marginal planting showing Mimulus cardinalis *and* Primula florindae.

CONTAINERS FOR MARGINALS

Care should be taken in the selection of containers and they should be fully compatible with the material from which the pond itself is constructed. With concrete ponds, brick or block troughs can be made at the time of construction, divided into sections of the correct size for each of the intended species. With fibreglass or sheet plastic, bought plastic troughs are best. Troughs should be about 9in (22.5cm) high, and two-thirds filled with a mixture of two parts good friable loam and one part well-rotted manure. Cover with about 2in (5cm) of pea gravel. This serves to stop the fish from disturbing the soil and clouding the water.

REED MACE *Typha latifolia*

Reed mace *Typha latifolia* is often mistakenly referred to as Bulrush. **Description** Long slender green leaves. The flower head consists of a collection of female flowers closely packed in a solid cylindrical cluster, 1in (2–3cm) in diameter and 4–6in (10–15cm) long, light chocolate-brown in colour, surmounted by a 6in (15cm) spike carrying the male flowers. One of the most useful materials for flower arranging. **Varieties** *T. minima*, Dwarf Reed Mace reaches only 1–2ft (30–60cm). It has smaller rounder flowers than *T. latifolia*. Ideal for the small pond requiring only 3–6in (15cm) of water, but it is not fully hardy and is therefore suitable for growing only in areas with mild winters. **Flowering season** Early to mid-summer. **Water depth** 6–36in (15–100cm). **Planting time and method** Plant a 6in (15cm) piece of the rhizome in humus-rich soil at least 8–10in (20–25cm) deep. **Cultivation** Cut back dead foliage in the autumn. **Propagation** Lift and cut the rhizome into segments during mid-spring.

grow out of control. It is far better to plant the marginals in containers; not only does this tend to slow down the growth, but it will also provide a finite boundary to the plant's terrestrial ambitions.

Design

A collection of marginals in the water is the equivalent of a herbaceous border on land and the same rules of composition will apply. This is often usually disregarded in the design of water gardens, and the collection appears as a jungle. The layout should be plotted out on paper, with the siting of the troughs, if these are to be permanent features (if not, they may be moved around as plant holders are in a patio). Site the marginals farthest from the viewing eye, so they do not obstruct the view.

A good basic design for the larger water garden is based upon the kidney shape; not only does this form engender interest in itself, but it has a large front area compared with the back, and an open front construction allowing the observer to see into the bed. It also allows the largest area in which to grow tall subjects without obscuring the view.

Allow 3ft (1m) in height for the 'backcloth'. A *Typha*, or Reed mace makes an excellent central subject, with irises, *Sagittaria* or *Peltandra* as the supporters. In front of these, three or four of the smaller species – *Calla*, *Caltha*, *Mentha aquatica* and *Myosotis* – are all suitable.

Choosing Plants

There is not a wide range of marginals, and the colours are less bright than with the terrestrial species, so there is far less danger of colour clashes within the bed. With the dark green of the vegetation, the water in the foreground, and the fact that the plants do not all flower together, this aspect may safely be ignored. This is not to say that the marginals cannot create dramatic effect – the Marsh Marigold, for example, should always be given sufficient room at the front of the display, as it greets the spring with a dazzling display of

KING CUP MARSH MARIGOLD *Caltha palustris)*

Varieties 'Alba' a white form, and 'Plena' a double yellow.
Description Butter-yellow, cup-shaped flowers 1in (2–3cm) across.
Height 1ft (30cm).
Flowering season Early to late spring.
Water depth 6in (15cm).

Planting time and method Plant in containers between mid-spring and early summer in a humus-rich soil.
Cultivation Remove dead material during the winter. Lift every two to three years and replace soil and single crown.
Propagation By crown division during the spring.

BOG ARUM *Calla palustris*

A British Native
Description Broad-leaved arum with a white oval spathe.
Height 3ft (1m)
Flowering season Early summer.
Water depth 2–6in (5–15cm)
Planting time and method Place in a basket filled with a slightly acid soil in early spring.
Cultivation Lift and replace soil as necessary.
Propagation By crown division during the spring, or by saving the seeds from the red berries and sowing in the spring in a peat-based compost which is kept permanently moist. Transfer to permanent site the following spring.

golden cups. You will almost certainly be restricted to only one water bed, and this will have to sustain interest throughout the year, so choose from the following plants to provide a succession of flowers from early spring to late summer.

Calla palustris (**Bog Arum**) This acquires its popular name from the white arum-shaped flowers which are pollinated by water snails. These are followed by red arum-type berries in late summer. A British native.

***Caltha* sp (Marsh Marigold, Kingcup)** Prefers a slightly acid soil (pH 6.0 – 6.5), rich in humus, such as would be found in its natural habitat. *C. palustris* 'Alba' is a white and *C. palustris* 'Plena' is a double yellow.

Iris kaempferi Arguably the most majestic of all marginals, irises adorn the edge of the pond as water-lilies do the middle. They flourish in 3–4in (7–10cm) of water. Flowers early summer, and may be obtained in shades of white and yellow. *I. laevigata* is slightly smaller than *I. kaempferi*, but is a true marginal, preferably about 4in (10cm) of water. It is of the deepest shade of blue, and there is a white variety, 'Alba'. The yellow iris seen in ponds and on river banks in the British countryside is *I.pseudacorus*.

*Gypsy wort and water mint (*Lycopus europaeus *and* Mentha aquatica*).*

THE WATER IRISES

*The yellow flag (*Iris pseudacorus*) flowers throughout June.*

A large group of arguably the most beautiful of all marginal plants, characterized by their tall stems and typical iris blooms. The three main species are *Iris kaempferi*, *I. laevigata* and Yellow Flag, *I. pseudacorus*. There are several sports.

I. KAEMPFERI

A native of the Far East.
Description Each stalk carries three or four flowers 6in (15cm) across a lead or terminal blossom which opens before the secondaries beneath it. The inner petals are short, being dominated by the broader outer ones. Colours: all shades of blue, often with a yellow streak and white.
Height 2½ft (75cm).
Flowering season Early to mid-summer.
Requirements May be grown at the edge of ponds or in boggy conditions. Requires a humus-rich soil and will not tolerate lime.

I. LAEVIGATA

A native of the Far East.
Description The three or four flowers are 4in (10cm) across with the inner and outer petals broadly of the same size. Colours: Deep blue with the outer petals having a white flash. Sub-species: include *I. albo-purpurea*, white with blue markings, and *I. semperflorens*, which produces blue flowers, both in early and late summer.
Height 2ft (60cm)
Flowering season *I. laevigata* and *I. albo-purpurea* early summer; *I. semperflorens* early to late summer, with dense clumps that may appear continuous.
Requirements Plant during the early spring in 2–6in (5–15cm) of water in humus-rich soil; will tolerate chalk soils.

I. PSEUDACORUS, YELLOW FLAG

Hardy native of Europe and UK.
Description Stems carry six flowers of bright mid-yellow flowers, with outer petals only slightly narrower than the inner. Colours: species is yellow; varieties tend to variations of this colour.
Height 3ft (90cm)
Flowering season Late spring and early summer.
Requirements Plant in 6–12in (15–30cm) of water in a humus-rich soil in early spring. It will develop large clumps which may be grown undisturbed for several years in a large pond, but will require regular lifting, dividing and replanting in more restricted sites. Tolerant of chalk.

Propagation of all Water Irises Lift and divide the rhizomes after flowering.

Mentha aquatica (**Water-Mint**) This prefers shallow water, and is almost a bog subject. It produces pinkish-blue flowers in late spring and early summer, and has a pleasant aromatic smell. It is very easy to cultivate.

Menyanthus trifoliate (**Bog-Bean**) A vigorous marginal preferring 2–3in (5–7cm) of water. Produces a carpet of pink flowers in late spring and summer. This plant has a spreading habit and it must be ruthlessly thinned each year, otherwise it

---

ARROWHEAD *Sagittaria sagittifolia*

Description It takes its name from the leaves which appear above the water and have an arrow-head shape; they are mid-green in colour with brown blotches. The stem carries a number of flat, white-petalled flowers with dark centres in groups of three at the top or along the stem centres, giving the appearance of small fried eggs.

Height 1½–3ft (45–90cm)

Flowering season Mid- to late summer.

Water depth 6–24in (15–60cm)

Planting time and method The foliage dies back at the end of the season leaving the underground tubers, which can be lifted and planted in early spring. The soil – which should be rich in humus – must be at least 6in (15cm) deep.

Propagation By lifting and dividing the tubers.

---

will take over the site completely.

***Myosotis palustris syn. M. scorpioides* (Water Forget-me-not)** This has a leaf and flower similar in shape to the terrestrial forget-me-not, but flowers in summer long after the latter has ceased, and at a time when there is declining interest in the water garden. This makes it a must for virtually all informal ponds. It is a British native.

***Peltandra* species.** Like the Bog Arum, to which this plant is closely related, *Peltandra* have arum-like flowers and berries. If this is the effect you are seeking, in the majority of small gardens you would be better advised to grow the smaller *Calla palustris*.

***Ranunculus lingua* 'Grandiflora' (Spearwort)** It is easy to see how the common name arose as this plant appears very much like a spear growing out of the water. It flowers early in mid-summer, producing golden-yellow buttercup-type flowers up to 2in (5cm) across.

***Sagittaria* (Arrowhead)** The leaves have the characteristic shape of an arrowhead. There are several different species but the one which is most commonly in cultivation is **S. sagittifolia**. It favours fairly deep water – 1–3ft (30–100cm), the white flowers occurring during mid-summer. Set out the small plantlets or rooted cuttings during mid-summer, and take care to remove excess roots annually, as this is a plant which can take over a pond. British native.

***Stachys palustris* (Marsh Woundwort)** A perennial plant with many leaves, producing red flowers towards the end of the season.

***Typha* sp. (Reed mace)** This plant is often mistaken for the bulrush. It is without peer for floral arranging and *T. latifolia* can grow in water as shallow as 6in (15cm) or as deep as 3ft (1m). In good rich soil its height can exceed 6ft (2m). It should be planted away from the observer, and in design terms it fulfils the same role as a tree in a garden, giving mass and height to the scene. This is another vigorous grower which, unless kept in check, will take over the whole pond, so it is not a subject for the smaller water garden layout. *T. latifolia* and *T. angustifolia* are both British natives.

Zantedeschia aethiopica Another of the water plants with an arum lily-type florescence. In the spring it has a white flower with a yellow centre. The variety 'Crowborough' is the one that is most frequently grown.

FLOATING PLANTS

These are plants whose leaves float on the surface of the water, usually with the roots moving freely in the water and absorbing nutrients from it. They have no anchorage.

CANADIAN WATERWEED
Elodea canadensis

Varieties No true varieties but *Largarosiphon major* is very similar, performs the same role, and should be treated in a similar manner.

Description Has central stem with many spike-like leaves emerging from it.

Height Long flexible strings will distribute themselves throughout the water. It does not grow above water level.

Water depth 2ft (60cm).

Planting time Throughout the spring and summer.

Propagation During the spring take a 1ft (30cm) piece of the weed and attach to its base a small piece of lead. Lower it into the water. The roots, whose sole role is one of anchorage, will form and the plant will soon establish itself.

Cultivation The plant is fast-growing and will rapidly take over the pond, so it should be lifted during the late summer and thinned out.

A SELECTION OF FLOATING PLANTS

Aponogeten distachyos **(Water Hawthorne)** The popular name is derived from the perfume that the plant emits. It has egg-shaped leaves which float on the water, and delicate pink and white flowers throughout the summer months.

Eichhornia crassipes **(Water Hyacinth)** This is one of the most beautiful of water plants, its popular name deriving from the pale blue hyacinth-like spikes of flowers. Unfortunately it is a tender subject and must be kept inside under frost-free conditions during the summer.

Hydrocharis morsus-ranae **(Frogbit)** Small white flowers.

Nuphar Yellow flowers not unlike a celandine, with both floating and submerged leaves. Flowers throughout the summer.

Nymphoides **(Floating Heart)** Not to be confused with the water-lilies Nymphaea. Yellow flowers from summer through till autumn. Tolerant of a wide range of water depths.

Trapa natans **(Water Chestnut)** This is a tender annual plant which is grown for its attractive leaves. It is propagated by seeds.

Water hawthorn (right) and frogbit (below).

CHAPTER 5

Pond Life

The charm of the water garden can owe as much to the life that it contains and – just as importantly – that it attracts, as it does to the plants that it supports. From the animal standpoint, ponds fall into two categories: those that are managed and depend upon fish for their interest; and those that are natural gardens relying upon the wildlife which finds it way in and around the water.

KEEPING FISH

The vast majority of pond owners will want to keep fish. These vibrant and often spectacular forms of life, one minute basking in the sun and the next darting about the pond like metal flashes, really are pets. Once they have confidence in their owners they will take food from the hand, and come at a

A carp can become very tame and eat from the hand.

Water-lily leaves provide goldfish with camouflage from predators and protection from the sun.

certain time of day to the part of the pond where they are accustomed to being fed. Fish always attract attention in any garden, whether it is a large landscape area or a small suburban patch. The Chinese, great pond builders, started the process of selective breeding to obtain the most spectacular forms of fish. This process has been greatly advanced in the twentieth century since the theory

SELECTING FISH FOR STOCKING A POND

1. Always obtain your stock from a reliable source, a good dealer will be happy to assure you which varieties are hardy. Fish obtained from fairgrounds, car boot sales, and itinerant traders may introduce disease into the pond even if they survive.
2. Never purchase fish that are contained within plastic bags. These containers are satisfactory for transporting fish over short distances but not for housing them for long periods.
3. Before purchasing, ensure that the fish are healthy: they should be free swimming, have no signs of

fungal infections or other growths, and should have no cuts or abrasions, both of which are sites of entry for disease. Select hardy, streamlined types that do not possess delicate, easily damaged fins.
4. When stocking a pond it is far more economical to purchase small fish. Given time, they will all become larger. Apart from being much cheaper, young fish can more readily adapt to a new home.
5. If there is need to replace fish, select specimens of similar size to those already in the pond.

of genetics has been understood, and we now have forms of goldfish that are far removed from their wild ancestors. Often, however, the most exciting types – the brightest-coloured, or those with the most elaborate fin structure – are the most difficult to raise, precisely because they are so far removed from the natural forms. Elaborate fin structures, for example, come at the expense of the speed necessary to catch prey in competition with other, more streamlined types. Similarly, they may lack the speed needed to escape a predator (the bright colours usually favoured by pond keepers offer no camouflage), or they may be incapable of withstanding the severest winter. Varieties such as the delicate fantails are an example.

Even the most difficult of fish can be raised if you make the effort and take the necessary steps to provide for their special requirements. Although bred in captivity for several generations, they will still retain the basic instincts of wild fish, still requiring places where they feel they can rest without the stress of constantly being on their guard against predators. Adequate cover can be provided by overhanging boundary paving or a submerged half-flower pot with the end open to form an artificial tunnel.

Winter

The majority of fish that are kept in ponds are members of the carp family. The breeding of ornamental carp originates from China, but the farming of carp in Britain dates back to at least the Middle Ages when they were raised for food. Their rearing and keeping usually presents no problem as most are able to withstand the harshest winters – some, noticeably the fantail, will require extra heat. During the winter months organic materials in the pond will continue to decompose as a result of bacterial action on the floor of the pond, resulting in a build-up of the gases methane, ammonia and the lethal hydrogen sulphide. At the same time, the fish will be using up the oxygen which is stored in the water. It is important, therefore, that even during the severest spells of cold weather an exchange of the gases can take place and a space is kept open. The most practical way of achieving this is to place an old tennis ball on the surface of the pond. The small currents and the wind will cause the ball to move about, and this movement will stop the water in that small area from freezing.

This alone will be effective in milder areas, and in all but the severest of winters, but there will be occa-

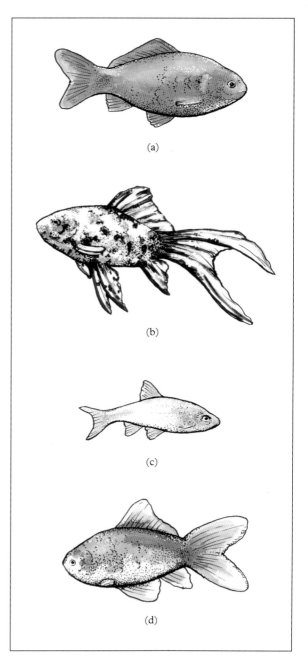

Four popular fish: (a) goldfish, (b) shubunkin, (c) golden orfe, (d) comet.

sions when the water freezes even around the ball. An ice-hole must be opened immediately, by clearing any snow away and pouring boiling water into a large tin resting on the surface to melt the ice. You must not attempt to crush the ice, as this will create compression waves in the water which may kill the fish.

A far more reliable method of saving your fish in the winter is to purchase a small electrical pond heater which can be connected to the mains. These are extremely economical to run, and are only switched on during a cold spell or when one is expected. They are not of course designed to raise

A wide variety of fish including Koi carp.

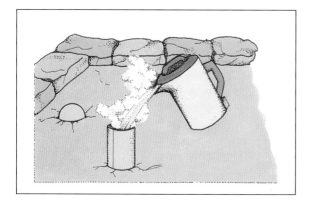

To make a hole in the ice sufficiently large for the escape of gases to take place, place a can on the surface and pour near-boiling water into it. The rubber ball relieves some of the pressure created by the ice.

the temperature of the whole pond, but only of a small area. The slight localised rise in temperature will ensure that a small hole remains open through the ice during even the coldest spells. This will be sufficient for the necessary exchange of gases to occur.

Stocking with Fish

The number of fish that you can keep will depend upon the quantity of oxygen dissolved in the water, which in turn will depend upon the depth; it is not the case that double the volume of pond water means that you can keep twice as many fish. A far better method to determine the number of fish which can be kept is based on the surface area of the pond. A large fish of about 6in (15cm) will use up approximately twice the oxygen of one half its size, but that small fish will, in time, grow to the full size for its species. To avoid over-crowding at a later stage, you should under-estimate the space available. You can always add extra fish. *Never have more than one fish per 2–3 sq ft (0.3 sq m)*. Koi carp grow much larger than many, and if you wish to raise them to full size you should not stock at a rate greater than *one fish per 20–25 sq ft (2–3 sq m)*. They are not a subject for the small garden pool.

Any sudden change in their environment leads to stress in fish, which can kill them or lower their resistance to disease. To avoid a sudden temperature change, allow the fish to remain in the transporting container and water until it reaches ambient temperature. Gently place the container and fish in the pond, tilting so that the fish may swim out.

Fish Breeding

Fish breeding is often thought of as an unplanned accident, however, with a little care and forethought, it is possible to increase your chances of successfully raising the young fish to adulthood. Few people will wish to raise their fish to exhibition standards – if you do then you will need to direct all of the pond's activity towards this aim, and you will require a good working knowledge of genetics. Most people will prefer simply to breed fish and dispose of them to the local pet shop.

The sexing of goldfish is so difficult for the inexperienced as to be virtually impossible. Whilst it is true that the male has tubicles (growths) on its gills, to see these it is necessary to catch the fish and move aside the perinitum, an operation that can damage the fish, and create a point of entry for disease. Immediately prior to breeding the female will become swollen with eggs, and viewed from above she will seem to be much wider than the male. However, the size of goldfish is a very complex matter, depending amongst other factors, on the nature of the environment. They are even capable of suspended growth – a goldfish can live for many years in an aquarium and never exceed about 2in (5cm), but on release into a pond will rapidly grow. (The reason for this is not fully understood, but the growth may be suspended as a result of the stress of living in an alien environment.) During the breeding season (which is dependent upon both the temperature and number of daylight hours, and runs from late April until August) it is possible to touch the female in the vent region, discharging a small quantity of eggs. The male will then emit a small amount of milk-like sperm.

Goldfish breed in groups and do not readily fight, so do not be worried about an over-provision of either sex. The best way of ensuring that you have both a male and a female is to include three fishes in the pond – the odds against having only one sex are one in four; if you have four fish then the odds are one in eight. Goldfish are ornamental carp, and the majority of carp will breed with each

Small goldfish bought from a pet shop will rapidly grow in a pond.

other. However, where the breeds are the same the chances of them breeding successfully are far greater. The common goldfish sold in pet shops is sufficiently hardy to survive our winters, and these same fish, so often thought of as only suitable for the aquarium, will happily breed in a pond. Ornamental fish are the result of selection and do not always breed true, and less colourful young may occur as recessive genes reappear in future generations. Should you wish to obtain fish that will breed true, ensure that you obtain your stock from a specialist supplier who will advise you on your needs.

For general pond breeding and building up a future healthy generation, it is advisable to obtain stock from at least two different sources. Unrelated fish will provide a large gene pool, which will produce hybrid vigour in the offspring, which will be better adapted to survival. In the natural world, there is a constant tendency to mix the genes for this reason.

Goldfish do have a breeding season, although a specimen trapped in a bowl in a centrally heated environment may not notice the passing of the year (another possible reason for the temporary suspension of growth). The pond dweller exposed to the elements will experience a slowing down of its metabolism with the shortening of the days and the onset of the colder weather. This is accompanied by a drop in the amount of food consumed: by midwinter the fish will be virtually fasting, living on the store of fat laid down during the summer. In the natural world this is the mechanism which allows the fish to survive when there is virtually no food available. Since this process is governed by the seasonal cycle, food provided at this time of year will not be consumed, but will sink to the bottom of the pond and decay. This rest period is very important for pond fish, which would otherwise become grossly overweight as a result of the abundant food supply.

With the onset of spring, the rising temperature and the longer periods of daylight trigger the start of the breeding cycle. For successful breeding, the fish should be placed in the pond by the previous autumn in order that the breeding groups are already established by the spring. Thereafter, every effort should be made to ensure that a stress-free environment is maintained.

During the spring or summer, when the female is swollen with spawn, the male will approach her and, by movements of his body near to hers, induce her to deposit the eggs on to nearby water weed, which are then externally fertilized. From the moment the spawn leaves the female's body it is in danger, falling prey to any adult fish and various other predators, so you need to spot the spawn as soon as it is laid (you may safely assume that it has been fertilized) and transfer it to an aquarium where the fry can be raised safely. Goldfish will eat their own eggs virtually as soon as they are laid, and this explains why the fish in some stocked ponds never increase in number. Occasionally one will survive the egg and fry stage, but overcrowding does greatly reduce the chances of the young surviving.

Goldfish do not usually spawn in temperatures below 59°F (15°C) and it is advisable to measure the temperature regularly during the spring. As it approaches the spawning temperature, look out for eggs each day on water weeds or the underside of floating plants. If you collect the eggs, you will have more than enough for your purposes. In the pond, no special food is required for young fish, which will readily feed of the minute organisms present, but in the aquarium special food available from pet suppliers must be provided.

Raising the Eggs

Inside every fertile egg there is an embryo which needs oxygen. This passes through the wall of the egg, with the waste gases passing out in the opposite direction. It is therefore important that the water is well oxygenated and, if you intend raising a large quantity of young, you will need an oxygenator (obtainable from most pet shops) for your aquarium. For small-scale fish rearing experiments (and it is always better to raise a smaller quantity than to risk losing all the young through over-crowding), simply set up the aquarium with gravel and water

weed in the usual way. The temperature of the water should be 65–70°F (18.5–21°C). Remember that in a pond fluctuations are only slight, compared with an aquarium, where there is far less volume of water, and a much greater surface area through which the heat can be lost following the slightest change in ambient temperature. The young will hatch after 4–5 days. Any eggs remaining 3 days after the first ones have hatched, or ones which have fallen to the bottom of the aquarium, will almost certainly be infertile and should be removed immediately before they begin to decay and pollute the water.

Raising the Fry

When the fry emerge they will have the yolk sac attached and this will be sufficient food for the first few days, but then you should provide the yolk of a boiled hen's egg. It is very important that you do not over-feed. Excess food will break down and use up some of the available oxygen. After a week of egg yolks, gradually provide other food, but only that which is small and soft. The goldfish should remain in the aquarium system until at least ten weeks old, and as they get older they will require additional quantities of oxygen. With large numbers of goldfish, either set up additional aquaria, or cull so that you are left only with those fish that have the best appearance. Once they have reached adulthood the young may be returned to the pond, but only if there is sufficient room.

Food for Goldfish

Fish will acquire much of the food that they need from natural sources. Minute crustacea, insects and mosquito lava all contribute to the diet, but you may need to supplement this. Give small amounts of any of the proprietary fish foods. Pelleted foods are compounded to provide an exact balance of the nutrients required, but take care not to over-feed. Provide no more food than you can comfortably hold between your thumb and forefinger. Ensure that the fish will eat all of it, and clear away any that is not consumed. Surplus food will rapidly begin to decompose and cause clouding of the water. This decomposition will release nitrogen and other minerals which will encourage the growth of micro-organisms causing further clouding.

Care must be taken not to over-feed fish.

Generally, the rate at which a fish grows and uses up food will depend upon the temperature, although above a certain temperature it will begin to slow down again. In addition, the fish will consume more food in the spring when they are producing eggs, but this will be partially compensated for by their tendency to eat their own eggs and by the abundance of wild food present. The summer will generally be a time of high food intake, due to the breeding season extending to August, and the building up of reserves for the winter. Because of the reduced metabolic rate during the winter months, providing the fish are healthy there will be no need to feed them, and they probably will not take food even if it is offered.

Fish can be trained virtually to take food from their owner's fingers. To train the fish, come to the pond at the same time each day. Hold a small quantity of food in your fingers at the surface of the water. Avoiding sudden movements release the food into the water. Do this over a period and, as the fish gain confidence they will eventually take the food from your fingers. This will also afford you the opportunity to check that the fish are healthy.

THE GOLDFISH'S YEAR

WINTER

General lack of activity, only slight movement; will not take food.

LATE WINTER/EARLY SPRING

Movement increases; will take first food.

LATE SPRING

Activity increases; initially there is an increase in the food which may be taken but this may drop off if there is an abundance of insects and other natural food. The first eggs may be seen.

SUMMER

Egg-laying may continue until mid-summer; on very warm days fish will tend to be less active and will temporarily eat less. If they come to the surface gasping for air it is a sign that there is insufficient oxygen in the water.

LATE SUMMER

Food consumption is now directed towards laying down the deposits of fat for the winter.

AUTUMN

Rate of food consumption gradually drops, along with activity.

Goldfish (*Carassius auratus*)

No fish is better suited to live with man than the goldfish. It can survive the ordeal of being transported from a fun fair in a small plastic bag and, after being unceremoniously deposited in a pond, may live for years. However, this is not a recommended way of obtaining your specimens. If they remain in such a bag for any period of time they will die through lack of oxygenated water, and fish from unknown sources always carry the risk of bringing disease with them. There is no substitute for buying your fish from a reputable dealer. As a bonus he will usually be able to provide any extra advice that you might require.

The goldfish is too well known to require any detailed description, with its metallic scales in a wide range of colours. Under ideal conditions it will grow to a maximum length of 4–5in (10–12cm). The common goldfish is the variety best suited to most ponds and will live trouble free for many years. Modern breeding has led to distinct varieties of goldfish.

There are many types of goldfish to choose from.

Shubunkins These have a gene missing, the one that is responsible for the metallic lustre, and they also carry the blue factor. This produces a range of apparently scaleless fish in a wide range of colours. They tend to be no more difficult to raise than the common goldfish and may be recommended to the novice fish keeper.

Comet This is a variety of the shubunkin, with a rear fin which can be almost half of the total length of the fish, and no anal fin. The more subdued colours, and the greater agility afforded by the modified rear fin, makes this a variety which is particularly well suited to survival; like all shubunkins it is hardy. This is another fish which can be recommended to all pond keepers.

Fantail This is a form of goldfish which retains the metallic sheen, with the distinguishing characteristic of an almost egg-shaped body curving into the downward-facing caudal fin. It is a fish of great beauty. However, it is not sufficiently hardy for Britain unless the pond is heated. It is sometimes suggested that this form can be transferred to an aquarium in winter, but this is not satisfactory as it can lead to different rates of growth, and because the fantail will soon outgrow all but the largest aquaria.

Veiltail A variety of the fantail with a far more elaborate caudal fin consisting of a series of folds. This slows the fish down considerably and makes it difficult to rear, so it should only be considered by the experienced fish keeper.

Golden Orfe This is one of the most streamlined of all species. A bright reddish-gold in colour, it is an ideal subject for the larger pond.

KOI CARP (*CYPRINUS CARPIO*)

These are great favourites in large gardens that are open to the public, where their colouring, size and darting movements provide constant interest. These Japanese fish can easily be raised at home, providing you have a sufficiently large and deep pond. If the conditions are ideal some may grow to almost 3ft (1m) in length, so they do require a fairly large pond! Because of their specialist requirements they cannot be recommended for an owner of a small garden pond. Even if you were able to provide a sufficiently large area of water, it is unlikely that you could provide a design capable of retaining the balance between a sufficiently large water garden and its surroundings. To prosper carp need room to move, and a depth of 4–5ft (1.5m) of water. Such a depth will prohibit the growth of some water-lilies, but it does open up the possibility of growing the spectacular *N. grandiflora*. The large fish, with their high energy movement, will metabolize large amounts of oxygen, only part of which can be successfully produced by water weeds. Providing you stock at a rate of no more than one fish per 20–25 sq ft (2–3 sq m) there is no need to aerate the water artificially, although it is advisable to provide a fountain. A significant amount of oxygen may also be obtained through a waterfall in the system. A fountain or waterfall should be working in the morning when the oxygen supply has been used up during the night.

Minnows (*Phoxinus phoxinus*)

For anyone who is interested in raising British native fish, the easiest to begin with is the humble minnow, which will only grow to about 3in (7–8cm) in length. The barrel-shaped fish prefers to live in a shoal and its darting movement appears as silver flashes in the water – a random movement that is totally coherent within the group itself. Over

---

SNAILS

Water snails will feed on any excess of food and the general detritus of the pond. These scavengers are essential if you are to have any hope of keeping the water clear.

Ramshorn snail (*Planorbis corneus*) is light brown, flat and coiled. It is totally hardy, available from all aquarium suppliers, and an hermaphrodite which will breed readily in your pond. It is the safest snail to have because, unlike other species, it does not graze off cultivated vegetation. However, the small white eggs, which soon develop black spots of the growing embryos and which are laid throughout the spring and summer, will often be eaten by fish and other predators.

Great pond snail (*Lymnaea stagnalis*) As well as feeding off dead and decaying material, this snail, which looks like a unicorn's horn, will graze off the vegetation. For this reason, it should never be included in any pond where there has been a planting of ornamental vegetation, especially water-lilies. However, the ramshorn snail, which feeds entirely on dead material, may be included in either type of pond.

Ultimately it is the food supply that will determine the number of snails that the pond will support. It will be about a year before a true balance is established, but for a medium-sized pond you should initially buy between three and five snails.

---

the years millions of these tiny fish have perished through lack of oxygen, as a result of being transported and kept in jam jars by eager youngsters. If they are quickly transferred from the wild to the garden pond they will immediately accept their new environment. During the spring the female will lay her eggs. These will hatch in 9–12 days and the shoal size will settle down to the maximum number that the size of the pool and the food can accommodate. Being natives they are perfectly hardy, although it will be necessary to remove the ice from the water during cold spells.

WATER WEEDS

If your pond is to sustain life, it must have water weeds growing in it. These are the plants which

Common duckweed. In other than a natural pond this is considered to be a weed and must be removed periodically.

oxygenate the water during the daytime. The role of the roots is one of anchorage, with nutrients being absorbed through the stem, and gravel is the ideal rooting medium. Fill a large ceramic flower pot with gravel and place pieces of water weed in the rooting medium. Carefully lower the container-grown plants into position. For water weeds to prosper they must be planted in a position that receives maximum sunlight. The amount of oxygen that the weeds produce will depend upon how much light can penetrate the water.

Callitrich piatycarpa (starwort) Can form an underwater jungle which should be cut back to manageable proportions each summer. Due to its vigorous growth, it is a useful plant for the larger pond.

Ceratophyllum demersum An oxygenator that can survive at depth, where less sunlight penetrates. Probably the best plant for shaded parts of the pond.

Elodea canadensis (Canadian pondweed) The most popular of all oxygenating plants. A prolific grower which spreads rapidly and which requires drastic cutting back during August and September.

Lagarosiphon major syn. Elodea crispa Very similar to *E. canadensis* in growth and habit.

Myriophyllum sp. A genus of oxygenating plants which produce small insignificant inflorescence

Whorled water milfoil.

above water level. *M. spicatum* has minute red flowers, and others lime green flowers. Not one of the better oxygenating families.

Ranunculus aquatalis (Common water crowfoot) As well as the submerged oxygenating parts, the plant also produces floating leaves and small yellow buttercup-shaped flowers during the summer.

THE NATURAL WATER GARDEN

Ponds are one of the fastest of all natural features to disappear from the landscape, and natural ponds built into gardens are a recent innovation, the contribution of man to the preservation of natural species under threat. The area covered by gardens

Natural water gardens are an important ecological aspect of the environment.

in Britain is in excess of a million acres and, if the wild life of the country is to survive and co-exist with man, it is imperative for urban gardens to be enticing for the creatures of the natural world. No area is too built up to attract wild life, and the importance of man providing help is beyond dispute. It has been estimated that the frog population of the British Isles is only one per cent of what it was before the Second World War, and this illustrates the uphill struggle facing certain species.

Wildlife gardens, whether terrestrial or water, do not happen by accident. It is not sufficient to create a pond, fill it with water, and expect it to look after itself. Algae will take over and, given time, some forms of life will start to inhabit it: winged insects, including those that spend part of their lives underwater, will find their way to the pond, as

Detail of the ecological garden on a smaller site.

*Brooklime (*Veronica becabunga*).*

will amphibians. But it will depend upon the distance of the nearest natural pond as to how long the process may take, and it may be several years before the pond realizes its full potential as a natural habitat. Wildlife ponds so established should not be thought of as environmental cheating. For centuries man has interfered with the landscape, harnessing it to serve his needs; and many of the so-called natural ponds were originally constructed by man for other purposes, such as the watering of stock, or started life as something else, such as hollows created during the excavation of gravel.

Insects such as the water soldier (Stratiotes aloides) *will soon colonize such an area.*

To achieve the best results from your pond in the shortest period of time, it will require managing and the introduction of various species. However, do not be too enthusiastic in your efforts to attract wild life into the garden: *never* raid a natural habitat for either adult endangered species such as amphibians or their eggs or young. Quite aside from being irresponsible and environmentally unsound, it is an offence in many parts of the world, including the UK, and carries heavy fines.

A natural pond is the same as a basic ornamental fish pond, with the fish omitted. This does not mean that the pond can be neglected, as even indigenous species will not survive where leaves are decaying. Your pond will require ecological management by which you seek to attract species into the garden. You do not have to make special provision, because many creatures will enter your garden of their own volition, but it does help. Plant water weeds to provide the necessary oxygen for the eco-system, and provide other plants, such as natural marginals and bog subjects. Again do not raid natural habitats, but seek out the specialist suppliers. The pond is a total environment with many long and complex food chains, so stocks of minute organisms – algae, water fleas and freshwater shrimps – will build up first, and then higher animals will gradually be attracted to the area. The process may be speeded up by taking samples of pond water from natural ponds, and adding these samples to the bulk of the water. Then transfer some natural weed to the pond. The aim is to attract visiting pond-loving species rather than to imprison; providing the conditions are right, you will ultimately attract at least some of the higher forms of pond life to the water. It is also possible on occasions legally to acquire either eggs or tadpoles when there is a site shortly to be developed or where there is an overstock in a particular area. Contact your local conservation society (find their address in the local library), and they will inform you of any nearby sources.

Once the pond is laid out it will begin to attract migrants – few at first (perhaps honey bees stopping for a drink), then butterflies and, with luck, a dragonfly. Caddis flies, with their several different forms, will all ultimately come to your pond, as will a wide range of birds. You may even attract a kingfisher. Your pond is the start of your own nature reserve.

The Amphibians

All the amphibians tend to spend the breeding season in or near to water. As the summer progresses they spend more and more time on land with a marked preference for damp ground. Young frogs linger near the area where they were tadpoles, but as they get older they will venture forth to colonise new areas. During October they start their annual hibernation under damp stones. Amphibians lay their eggs in water and these hatch into tadpoles (or efts, in the case of newts), which metamorphose into the adult form in a matter of weeks. They are all carnivores, frogs consuming large quantities of slugs and harmful insects, and newts eating mainly insects and worms. Both, therefore, are extremely useful in the totally organic garden where no pesticides are employed.

Common frog (*Rana temporaria*) This is the only frog that is likely to find its way into your garden, and during March it may be heard croaking on the pond. Its breeding season is from March to May, when it lays its eggs in clumps, once the temperature has reached 48°–50°F (9°–10°C).

Common toad (*Bufa bufa*) This is the only other frog-like creature that you are likely to encounter in the garden, and it is readily distinguished from the frog by the large number of warts all over its body. The toad lays its eggs in long strings about a month after the frog has started, and they seem to get caught up in the water weed. Whether the frog or toad will be the more common in your garden depends upon the locality.

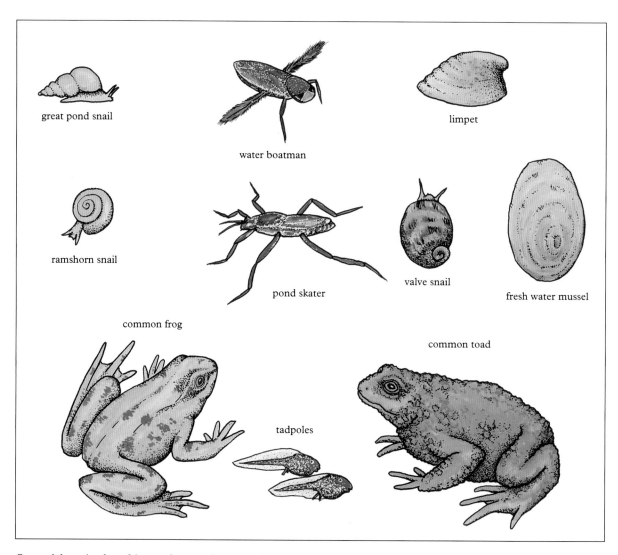

great pond snail

water boatman

limpet

ramshorn snail

pond skater

valve snail

fresh water mussel

common frog

common toad

tadpoles

Some of the animals and insects that may be attracted to your pond.

Great crested newt (*Triturus cristatus*) The rarer of the two British native newts, this is the larger and the male has a spectacular crest running along its back. Its breeding period lasts from March through to June. It is by no means unknown in garden ponds, but its appearance should be considered as a bonus rather than something which can be planned.

Smooth newt (*Triturus vulgaris*) As its scientific name implies, this is the common newt (although despite its name is becoming increasingly rare), and the one you are most likely to attract into your garden. It is only two-thirds of the size of the great crested newt. Newts tend to stay near water far longer than frogs and are amongst the most interesting of the natural pond creatures.

Frogs, toads and newts seldom prosper in the same pond, especially a small one, probably because they are all competing for the same food supply. Artificial introduction of any of these species is best achieved at the tadpole stage.

Other Creatures

Water stick insect (*Ranatra linearis*) A long, thin insect which preys on the other insects and tadpoles. The adults can both swim and fly and will rapidly colonise any pond. It should not be considered a pest, as it helps to maintain the balance of nature and destroy those herbivores which would feed off the vegetation.

Water boatman (*Sigara lateralis*) This is a very common brown-black insect which flies at night. There is also the common corixa which is often referred to as a water boatman. The latter is an oval-shaped insect with a steel blue body, which goes to the surface to breathe and seems to be suspended by the surface tension.

Water scorpion (*Nepa cinera*), **Saucer bug** (*Ilyocaris cimicoides*), and **water singer** (*Micronecta poweri*) These may all appear in any pond, although the larger the pool the greater the variety of these and similar species.

Caddis fly (Trichopterous sp.) These insects, of which there are several species, are somewhat similar in appearance. Of particular interest is the caterpillar which often has a tubular case to protect it, covered with grains of sand, twigs and various natural debris, effecting a camouflage.

Beetles and spiders There are several species of both of these which live either in or around water. The most fascinating is probably the water spider (*Argyroneta aquatis*), which builds a diving bell of silk which it then fills with air. It lives, mates and lays its eggs within this diving bell. The common pond skater (*Gerris lacustris*) is to be found on virtually every pond. The adult is unable to fly, so it uses the surface tension, and literally walks on water. The little pond skater (*G. argentatus*) and the tolland pond skater (*G. odontogaster*) both have a similar appearance and life-style, and are also very common. The water measurer (*Hydrometra stagnorum*) and lesser (*H. gracilenta*) are similarly surface dwellers which are widely distributed.

Mussels Freshwater mussels are vegetarians living mainly on algae and will obviously not survive unless there is an adequate supply. For this reason mussels should only be placed in an established pond where they will help in the maintenance of clear water. The mussel most frequently added to the garden pond is the highly attractive 'painter's mussel'. These can be purchased from a limited number of specialist suppliers.

CHAPTER 6

Other Features

MOVEMENT

The water garden should be seen in terms of the landscape as a whole and the contribution it makes to the total vista, and water is indispensable in a landscape because it is capable of providing both movement and sound. In large gardens, professional designers exploit the beauty of moving water to the full, providing dazzling displays of fountains and waterfalls. A similar effect is possible in the small garden providing attention is paid to the scale and balance of the plot. It is not impossible to design a garden without the element of water, but it is unlikely that the fullest potential of the site will be realised if it is omitted.

Natural rises and slopes that the designer chooses not to level are obvious sites for a waterfall, and where such natural contours do not exist they can

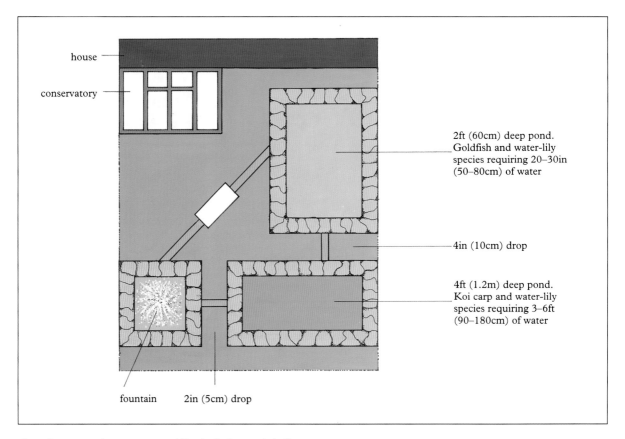

house

conservatory

2ft (60cm) deep pond. Goldfish and water-lily species requiring 20–30in (50–80cm) of water

4in (10cm) drop

4ft (1.2m) deep pond. Koi carp and water-lily species requiring 3–6ft (90–180cm) of water

fountain   2in (5cm) drop

A total water garden concept providing both deep and shallow water.

THE ADVANTAGE OF MOVING WATER

❀ Creates movement and interest within the garden.
❀ Will increase the dissolved oxygen in the water on a warm summer day.
❀ Increases the humidity, creating a better environment for ferns.
❀ It is less likely to freeze in winter.

be created artificially, from the material excavated in the building of the pond (*see* page 25). One approach is to attempt to create a watercourse reminiscent of an alpine scene with the whole of the area almost covered in granite or limestone. Less ambitious but equally effective visually is to rely on splash trays to drop the water to a lower level. All watercourses depend upon the ability to lift water, and the most fundamental of all questions that any gardener must ask himself is how high he wants to raise it. In any aspect of garden design it is important to maintain proportions. In the typical modern small urban garden 2½–3ft (60–100cm) is the maximum rise from the level that may be achieved and still retain the balance. The higher the water has to be raised the more powerful the pump that will be needed; this will affect both the initial costs and the running costs. Even the most modest fountain will require the movement of a large quantity of water. A simple, small single-jet system will emit about 1 gallon (4.5 litres) of water per minute.

When it comes to siting water features, it is possible to date the building of the garden from certain details. Up until recent times fountains were always sited at the centre of the pond, with no other position being considered suitable. Modern design allows for a far greater degree of individuality and features are now placed at the discretion of the creator. The water garden should be seen in terms of a picture where the eye will slavishly travel to a position one-third of the distance from the foreground, where the pond is constructed along a direct line from the point of observation to the back of the plot. Where the construction is at 90 degrees to this line then the split should be one-third to two-thirds from either end.

Designing features such as waterfalls and fountains into the system before it is built will enable you to insert the tubing carrying the water at the preliminary building stage, rather than burying it when it becomes a more complicated task. It is important to use top-quality tubing: copper tubing

A water garden with plenty of movement, surrounded by rockery plants such as Armeria mimula (*which also thrives in bog conditions*), *and* Campanula.

is the most suitable for buried structures; do not apply false economies by using cheaper hose which may split, requiring you to dig out the whole structure and relay it.

Outlets

The outlets for falling water are many and varied. Once the water has been raised it will of course fall, and you are free to direct it to do so in any way you choose. Each year accessory manufacturers have become more ingenious in their designs, with tumble trays, watercourses, water dispensers and fountains, and the kits to make them becoming available. In addition, the home handyman may create his own effects, from the classical to the ultra-modern, from the obvious to the ingenious.

Pumps

All water is lifted by means of a pump, which draws the water through the inlet, to which a filter must be fitted to ensure that there is no danger of the system being blocked by debris. A piston then pushes the water out under pressure. The height to which the water will rise will depend upon both the pressure and the size of the hole through which it is being forced – the smaller the diameter of the hole, the higher the jet will rise. Relatively great height may be achieved with a fountain, less with a waterfall. If you are using very small holes to produce height in a fountain, it is important to check that the jet is clear after it has been out of use for any period. Algae and other forms of growth will cause blockage, so be prepared to service the equipment regularly.

Moving water should not be over-done. Not only can it be visually confusing, but the demands can be far greater than the pump can handle, and this will shorten its life. An effective small watercourse will require the raising of gallons of water per hour and this will only be achieved if the pump is the correct one for the job. It does not matter how many steps there are on a watercourse, whether the water crashes down from well-defined shelves or meanders gradually down a slope, it is the height to which the water must be raised that governs the pump's capacity. Once it is released from the pipe, the pull of gravity takes over. A reputable dealer, or one of the increasing numbers of garden centres that are providing specialist water garden sections will be able to advise you on your individual requirements. Gardens are creations that

A watercourse created with simple, rough-hewn logs.

The flow of water, using a surface pump to create a watercourse and a fountain simultaneously.

need individual and unique consideration and planning, so it is essential that you discuss your requirements at the design stage. Do not delay until part of the water garden has been built or you might find that what you wished to achieve is impossible, or will be far too expensive in initial outlay or running costs. Only by careful planning will you avoid later disappointment.

Before you visit a supplier it is advisable to understand the difference between the two main types of pump on the market.

Surface Pumps The surface pump is situated outside the pond itself, and one of the main problems associated with it is the housing it needs to protect it. This has to be near to the water to reduce the inlet length of pressure tubing, and yet in such

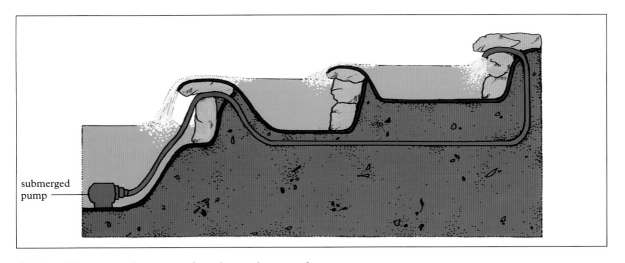

A submersible pump used to create a three-tier running-water feature.

Rocks and water coming together to produce an easily maintained part of the garden.

Fitting of Pumps

For any pump to function with the greatest efficiency it is essential that the correct hoses and fittings are used. It is also almost as important to ensure that water is moved through the minimum possible distance in the horizontal plane as in the vertical plane. Any movement means that the water will have to move against the friction of the system, and the resultant drag will make demands on the total performance of the pump, causing it to be less effective in raising the water. This factor must always be taken into account when siting a surface pump in order to maintain maximum efficiency of the pump.

a position that it does not create a visual intrusion which could spoil the whole effect. Concealment by means of rocks or strategically placed permanent plants should be sought.

Submersible Pumps These have the advantage that they are simply placed in the pond itself, eliminating the need for both inlet tubing and housing. The pump should be placed on a permanent level structure as near to the surface of the pond as possible, but where there is no danger of the inlet becoming exposed which could lead to an airlock in the system. Do not place it too deep in the water. For any pump, the height which it will be capable of raising a fixed volume of water will be limited, and to achieve the most dramatic effect the largest amount of the lift should be created *above* water level.

Submersible pumps present no problems and for small movements are probably the most convenient.

However, where large volumes of water are to be moved through a relatively great height, surface pumps have the advantage.

Splash Trays

The size of your garden and the need to lift the water will restrict the height of the waterfall. The most effective way to use water is to have two trays with lips over which the water will cascade. Trays like this will produce the greatest effect in terms of the water moved, but it is important to ensure that they are situated in a position where they will be lost in the general background. Whilst the two-tray approach is the simplest of all waterfalls, the most complex is little more, using the same cascading trays camouflaged as part of a grander scheme. The observer is misled into believing that this is a watercourse flowing naturally through the terrain. You must be careful not to end up with an insignificant trickle, and for this reason the cascading trays need a small yet definite functional lip over which the whole of the flow is directed. This results in the most sound and the best visual effect for the volume of water being moved.

Cascading trays may be purchased in a variety of plastics, and you should choose a set which does not possess too artificial an appearance. Where the trays are completely hidden within the design, the material is far less important. One design which is becoming increasingly popular is where there is a mound of earth, with two trays, a pond and medium-sized pieces of rock placed in the soil. A large variety of plants may be grown in the intervening space. In such a design the appearance of the dropping trays themselves is particularly important, and if you cannot obtain trays that blend visually with your scheme, you should consider making your own. The trays themselves need to be about 3in (7.5cm) deep so that they can hold sufficient water. Make a suitable cast, and mould the trays (which need to be about ½in (1cm) thick from a mixture of two parts cement, one part sand, peat or soil to blend with the surroundings, and four parts fine sand. Experiment with different blends – providing the cement ratio is maintained you may adjust the amount of sand and fillers until you obtain the shade you require. Where you are using a soft sandstone for the rock part, some of it may be ground down to produce the correct shade. Ensure that the trays have lips 2–3in (5–7cm) in length, protruding ½in (1cm) over the side. Where cement-based trays are being used it is important to realise that they are liable to breakage as a result of frost; rainfall should be emptied out of them during the winter months to avoid this problem.

Setting up the Trays

You will need two trays in addition to the pond itself. More ambitious schemes involving extra trays will almost certainly be impractical in the small garden, both in terms of visual effect and the expense of installing and running a sufficiently powerful surface pump. The hose from the pump will deliver water to the top tray, which is the smaller of the two, set at 8–12in (20–30cm) above the intermediate tray, which should be at a similar distance above the pond. It is very important that the two trays should be set absolutely level into a firm base and care should be taken to ensure that they cannot move. If necessary, they can be locked into position by the strategic placing of stones underneath.

Waterfalls

Although such a feature is contrived, it will never appear so artificial as to be out of place in any garden. However, should you wish to have a setting which appears almost completely natural, a full waterfall must be built. The mechanics of lifting the water and allowing it to fall will be the same, but the presentation will be different. Build a mound to the back of the pond where you wish the waterfall to be constructed and ensure that it is firm. Any movement as a result of subsidence at some stage in the future could result in the total destruction of the watercourse. The next stage is to cut two steps 8–12in (20–30cm) in depth, and cover these with a 2in (5cm) layer of concrete. The upright sections should be made with shuttering. Whilst the cement is still wet the cascading trays should be placed in position, and surrounded by rocks, both for concealment and to create the illusion of a mountain scape. There are several variations on the theme that you can create.

It is possible to create a very natural looking waterfall by using rocks to conceal cascading trays.

Flowering rush, Butomus umbellatus.

The combined effect of the pond and the falling water creating its own vapour is that the air in the vicinity is moisture-laden – the ideal microclimate for cultivating ferns. Ferns are amongst the oldest and most curious plants that have survived on the planet. They do not form seeds, but propagate themselves from a more primitive reproduction system – spores. These can be purchased from many seedsmen and are grown in a similar manner to seeds. Established ferns may be grown in pots and placed by the side of the waterfall, and then brought inside during the winter. The hardy varieties may be planted in a permanent position.

BUILDING A WATER COURSE STEP-BY-STEP

CAUTION Never perform electrical wiring near a water system unless you are fully qualified to do so. Water when combined with electricity is a potential killer.
1. Design the whole water garden accurately, deciding the height to which you wish to raise the water.
2. Visit garden centres to compare pumps. Establish which is the most suitable pump for the task, together with the running cost.
3. Construct the lower pond, leading the hose out of the pond and above the liner. Conceal the outlet with rock or similar material.
4. Lay the tubing and continue to the position immediately below the point where the water is to be discharged. Conceal discharge position with a piece of rock.
5. Employ a qualified electrician to connect the pump to the mains supply.
6. Complete the task by adding rocks or logs to create the illusion of a natural feature.

Moving Water and Life

Fish will be attracted to water containing the maximum amount of oxygen, and they will tend to congregate near a fountain to take in the air-enriched liquid. However, they must be able to spend the majority of their life in still water. Where moving water is included in a small area, such as the two heights of a patio, it may not be possible to provide the necessary environment for the fish. A sufficiently large area of water, on the other hand could well be out of balance with the overall scheme. Irrespective of whether the water is still or moving, the fish must be provided with a place where they may shelter away from the direct sunlight. This may be provided by including an overlay, or placing a land drainage pipe or half a large flower pot at the bottom of the pond. Where two or more ponds are interconnected the fish will be able to retreat between the connecting pools.

Plants do not generally prosper in moving water – many subjects which grow in rivers never succeed many feet away from the banks. At the river bank the rate at which the water flows is far slower than it is at the centre, due to the natural drag.

FOUNTAINS

Building a fountain is much easier than building a watercourse as it does not involve the installation of external fittings. Simply connect the exit point a short distance from the submerged pump. The fountain itself may be seen to emerge from a variety of orifices concealed in ornamental casements. Note: The water jet should emerge only just above the surface of the water as the main force of the pump must be used to pump up the invisible jet of water. The total height to which the water can be raised is determined by the power of the pump and, if most of the height is hidden within the structure of the fountain itself, much of the effect will be lost.

Statuettes with water being continually emitted from pitchers or pans work on the same principle as a waterfall, with the ornaments simply presenting the dispersal points.

LIGHTING

As gardens become smaller the tendency is to appreciate them more, and to seek ways to maximize the pleasure that can be derived from them. Sitting out in the evening from July through to September can be greatly enhanced by floodlighting the pond. Providing that you buy floodlights that are purpose-built for gardens, the installation is simple. However, *do* recognize the dangers of the combination of water and electricity and employ a competent professional. With a little experimentation and adjustment you will soon find the position which gives you the best effect, showing the water garden to its best advantage, making everything seem more spectacular, and creating magical reflections in the water. One of the best advantages of lighting a garden is the fact that you can sit and watch the numerous caddis flies and moths on the wing, and enjoy the beautiful evening perfumes of honeysuckle, stocks and *Nicotiana*.

BRIDGE BUILDING

A bridge within a water garden is symbolic, separating one part of the water garden from another, and giving an impression of mass and a degree of cohesion to the whole. Bridges do not demand vast areas nor deep water to span, but simply serve the same purpose as the pergola in a dry garden, linking two distinct parts. A bridge will only achieve this effect if it is built between, say the foreground and the background, or a grassed area and a bog garden, and it will not work in visual terms if it is constructed purely as an ornament. This does not mean in practical terms that the bridge should be the sole access to a particular part of the garden. It is far preferable to use the bridge only for occasional journeys (especially if you do not feel confident with the brick or woodwork necessary to produce a full load-bearing structure). With smaller water gardens you may build a bridge in proportion, and it may be totally impractical to use as a garden thoroughfare.

Consideration must be given to the materials of construction, which must harmonise with the facade of the house, the outbuildings, and, if appropriate, the materials of the water garden itself. A wooden bridge will fit in with all schemes, and there are basically two types – planed wood or rustic. With its more regular shape and the greater ease with which it can be preserved, planed wood

WOOD AND WATER

Wood above water will be constantly damp, creating the ideal conditions for rot and fungal infections, so it is imperative that the wood is constantly inspected and treated with preservatives. This year's neglect will lead to next year's decay. There are many different wood preservatives on the market, which will all produce a different shade; it is better to seek out a natural shade than the stark black of the old-fashioned creosote. Rustic finishes present a special problem as much of their charm is due to the presence of the bark. This soon comes away from the wood and, whilst preservative is readily absorbed, this does nothing to protect the layer below which is responsible for the strength of the structure. This layer will be particularly vulnerable to attack by woodlice and honey fungus. With rustic constructions it is far better to remove the bark first wherever this is possible, or as soon as is practical. All wooden structures should also be inspected regularly to ensure that the joints are secure – this will avoid the possibility of any accidents.

BUILDING A BRIDGE STEP-BY-STEP

joint formed between
the flat area and
approach/exit steps

main load-bearing joint

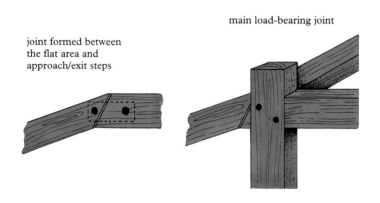

side framework

basic bridge without the sides

A bridge must consist of a solidly constructed walking area, which is common to all designs. Once this has been created a variety of facings can be added.

1. The bridge will be supported by two pairs of upright load-bearing posts or members, which should be pre-treated with wood preservative to protect them from water and weather, and then encased in a metal shoe. Place one pair on one side of the water to be bridged. The distance between these two posts will determine the width of the bridge, which in most cases is about 2ft (60cm). Place the other pair of posts on the opposite 'bank'. In each case, position the posts so that there is no risk of their damaging the membrane of the pond. Screw 2 × 2in (5 × 5cm) cross-members to the main supports, joining one of each pair of load-bearing uprights. To provide extra support place a right-angle metal bracket under the joint.

2. Prepare the floor of the bridge by making a 2 × 2in (5 × 5cm) frame cover, with ½in (1.5cm) floor board and screw these to the cross-members.

3. Place secondary members 3ft (1m) away from the bank on both approach sides. Join these to the main uprights and screw pieces of 2 × 2in (5 × 5cm) wood into position to make the approach steps.

4. The sides are made last and should be prepared by making a frame 4ft (120cm) high by the length of the bridge. Many different designs or patterns can be attached to this frame.

5. Screw the side frames to the base.

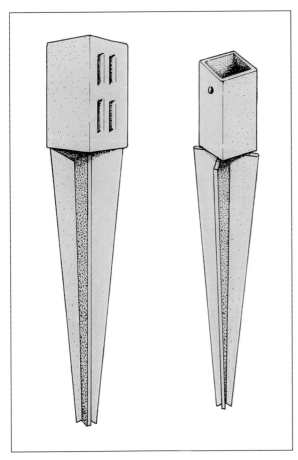

Steel post supports for supporting uprights on either side of the pond.

is best in the majority of cases. The uprights are easier to construct with sufficient mechanical strength and they are less inclined to become rickety as they get older. Safety and the avoidance of accidents must be a major consideration in the building of bridges. A bridge is an all-weather structure, which must be capable of withstanding the ravages of the elements. Second-hand timber from a demolition site is ideal. Not only will it be far cheaper than the equivalent new material, but you can be assured that it is well seasoned – an important factor. Rub any excessive roughness smooth with a sanding attachment to the electric drill, and fill any nail holes with putty – they will be totally invisible when the wood is covered with preservative.

The framework of the bridge should be bolted together to ensure maximum strength. The floor of the bridge must be made from ¾in (2cm) or thicker boards, and the structure above the floor may be either 2 × 2in planed wood or rustic poles – larch is the most usual.

The bridge may have a suggestive role in which it creates an illusion. In the ornamental garden, for

Providing that you construct a strong base and floor, bridges can be made load bearing with a variety of different side structures. Here a rustic design is used to fit in with a cottage or informal garden.

A bridge with woven sides adds character and additional interest to this garden pond.

example, plywood may be placed on the sides of the wooden bridge and painted with a design. This is particularly appropriate if you are attempting to produce a Japanese garden. This type of garden can be enhanced by the addition of a pagoda, which can double as a purely functional device, such as a shed or store.

Very elaborate brickwork structures may also be created, but building an arch is one of the most dif-

ficult skills of a bricklayer, and you should not attempt it unless you are proficient. One of the most sympathetic of all structures is a small stone bridge reminiscent of one of the little bridges across a Pennine stream. However, this again should not be attempted unless you have the necessary experience.

One very simple structure to build has a pillar on either side of the water, created out of rock cemented together in sheets. A plank is placed across the pillars and the level checked with a spirit level (any slight errors can be corrected later by adjustments to the thickness of the cement layer). Next, a large sheet of granite about 2in (5cm) thick is placed across the two pillars and cemented into position, and the level is then checked again. Whilst such a structure gives the illusion of a primitive rock bridge in either an alpine or a Pennine-type landscape, it will not be safe to walk on.

Any maintenance or repairs that are necessary from time to time will be best effected by placing planks across the water adjacent to the bridge, and working from these.

STEPPING STONES

These are an alternative to a bridge – a path through the water – and may be created by anyone. even when dealing with the shallowest water, you should place them in position before putting the water into the pond. It is possible to construct step-ping stones from any depth, but there is always an element of danger. The moist conditions will encourage the growth of micro-organisms and the stones will soon become slippery. Ensure that the water on either side is as shallow as possible if they are to be used for crossing. Where you do not want to use the stones, the only consideration is the visual effect, then the stones and water may be as deep as you like.

A straight line is the shortest distance between two points, and one of the aims with stepping stones (or any type of path) is to give the illusion of length – the impression that the aquascape covers a greater area than it really does. The eye will follow the line of the stones rather than seek out the shortest distance, and it is this that gives the impression to the observer that the area is larger than it really is. The effect can be achieved by laying the stepping stones in an almost straightened–out letter 'S' configuration, with the long backbone traversing the water diagonally and in the process joining the two focal points of the area.

A large flat stone cemented to pillars constructed from smaller pieces of stone make a very effective stone bridge.

CHAPTER 7

Seasonal Care and Management

Once established, ponds tend to be trouble free, but there is some routine management which is necessary.

SPRING

The conscientious pond-keeper will monitor the subtle changes that occurs in the pond's environment at this time of the year. Keep a careful watch for fish beginning to recommence their activity.

Very small amounts of food may be given, and that which is not consumed should be removed. When all the food is being eaten, the quantity may be increased.

Keep a look out for the first appearance of fish eggs on the underside of leaves or water weed. These should be transferred to an aquarium. Frog spawn appears as long strings of gelatinous eggs, toad spawn as single eggs on leaves; in both cases the eggs have black centres which develop into the embryonic tadpoles.

Marsh marigold – the herald of spring. The brown spikes are the previous season's growth of reed mace left to show the relative positions of the shorter and taller subjects in the bed and the manner in which the continuum of interest develops from the front to the back.

Pond Cleaning

All ponds require periodic cleaning. The frequency with which this is carried out will depend to some extent on the size of the pond: small ponds will require more regular cleaning than large ones. As a matter of course, leaves and other debris should be removed as soon as they enter the pond; where this has not been done the water will need cleaning out more frequently. Generally there is no need to clean a pond so long as the water is clear; the presence of decaying vegetation, which with time will inevitably accumulate at the bottom of the pond, increases the need for cleaning. Do not confuse decaying vegetation with green water, which is the result of algae and must be dealt with as outlined in Chapter 3 by restoring the balance of the pond. Cleaning is necessary only when the water is becoming progressively more hostile to life. If stirring the water dislodges debris at the bottom, cleaning should be carried out.

CLEANING A POND STEP-BY-STEP

EQUIPMENT

❀ Aquarium or other suitable container for fish
❀ Fishing net
❀ Buckets
❀ Large piece of muslin
❀ Brush
❀ Shovel or scoop
❀ Wheelbarrow

There are two methods of cleaning a pond.

METHOD 1

1. Catch the fish with the net and place them in an aquarium
2. Remove water weed and place it in the buckets filled with water.
3. Set aside another bucket of water to hold other beneficial forms of pond life such as snails.
4. Scoop the water out of the pond, pass it through the muslin and then discard it. Examine material on the muslin for any forms of life which can be placed with others in an appropriate bucket.
5. Remove the roots and crowns of marginals and water-lilies.
6. When the pond is empty of water, remove the debris from the bottom and place it in the wheelbarrow for transporting to the compost heap.
7. Sweep or sponge out the bottom of the pond. (There is no need to wash or treat the liner.)
8. Divide and replant water-lilies and marginals (see Chapter 4). Plant water weed.
9. Let water trickle into the pond from a hose pipe. Allow a couple of hours for any chlorine to disperse, before returning the fish.

Note: Fish require the same amount of oxygen whilst they are in their temporary home as they need in the pond itself, and very large specimens will need housing only one to a bucket. Even so, they may soon exhaust the oxygen supply and will require returning to the pond as soon as possible. This is usually safe providing that you are satisfied that there is no excess chlorine present which only usually occurs following works on the mains. (If excess chlorine is present in the water, you will be able to smell it.)

10. Before returning the fish conduct a routine examination to ensure that they are not damaged in any way and that there are no signs of fungal growths on the bodies or fins. If there are any problems isolate the individual fish by keeping it in an aquarium where it can be treated. Return it to the pond when it is fully recovered.

METHOD 2

This second method is a far less time-consuming operation than that discussed above in that it does not require you to empty the pond completely; rather, it involves changing one third of the pond's water. If routine management is good, and the pond is healthy, this method is a suitable alternative if carried out annually, when plant division can also be done. However, whatever the nature of the pond, it will be necessary to empty and clean out the pond completely at least once every ten years.

1. Remove the dead or decaying vegetation.
2. Pump out, or manually remove, one third of the total volume of water. Make sure that you take the water from the upper part of the pond so that you do not disturb the aerobic/anaerobic microbe balance. Inspect the fish for any health problems.
3. Re-fill the pond with a slow steady trickle of water in order not to disturb and distress the fish. Ideally, the water should originate from a water butt used to collect rainwater, but if this is not available you may use tap water.

A spring bog garden with Lysichiton americanum *and young fern fronds.*

RAISING FROGS AND TOADS

1. Remove the eggs, along with sufficient pond water to fill the aquarium.
2. Add a quantity of water weed to the aquarium.
3. When the small tadpoles hatch they will cling to the weed from which they will obtain their food in the early stages. At a week old, provide a small quantity of finely chopped hard-boiled egg. Immature tadpoles breathe through gills, but the tadpole's respiration gradually transfers to the lungs. Before this stage is reached, rocks or other suitable items that will protrude above water level must be placed in the aquarium to provide the young frogs with a place to rest and breathe.
4. When the tail has completely disappeared, the frogs may be taken and placed by the side of the pool.

Aim to perform the cleaning operation in autumn or early spring. In the latter case marginals and water-lilies can be lifted and divided at the same time.

Before attempting to clean a pond consider the material from which it was constructed and take the appropriate precautions to avoid damage. Ponds are most liable to be damaged during cleaning, especially those made from fibre glass or plastic.

Dividing Plants

Water-lilies and most marginals need dividing every three to four years and it is usually most convenient to replant them as part of the routine pond cleaning. If you adopt method 2 for cleaning the pond, water plants should be lifted and replanted every three years, although any species that start to dominate in the interim can be lifted and divided in the spring as necessary.

SUMMER

Feeding

Provided that the plants are not overcrowded and were planted in good rich loam there should not be a mineral deficiency and there will be no need to provide extra nutrients. However, where the plants fail to perform to the required standard, specially compounded pond fertilizers can be provided. Never use general land fertilizers or foliar feeds with pond plants, as these provide a rich excess of nutrients which results in a rapid build up of green algae in the water. Pond fertilizers are especially compounded to be higher in phosphates and potassium, and lower in nitrogen; they will be made from only partially soluble salts to allow them to dissolve slowly over a prolonged period and are often embedded in clay so that they sink to the bottom of the pond. Keep a sharp look out for aphids, water-lily beetles and china-mark caterpillars, which should be removed by spraying with a jet of water.

Fish

In warm weather, run the waterfall or fountain to aerate the water and provide extra oxygen for the fish.

Continue to keep a look out for fish eggs, which may be laid late into the summer. If left, they will seldom survive: even if they escape their cannibalistic parents, the fry will lack the reserves of energy to sustain them through the winter. But they can be raised inside in an aquarium for returning to the pond next year. Continue to feed the fish throughout the summer, giving only as much as they will take and removing the excess.

BEWARE!

Hot weather will evaporate the water; keep filled by allowing water to enter from a tube or via the hose.

A water garden with a subtly toned colour scheme.

The stately iris commands the margins in June.

Clearing the Water

During the summer, make preparation for the next year's work. If the water-lilies are less vigorous and their growth smaller than in previous seasons, overcrowding, a lack of nutrients, or a combination of the two is indicated. They must be removed and thinned out. Whilst this can be performed during the flowering season it is far better to delay until the following spring when the new buds can start afresh to produce strong viable tissue.

Summer can see the development of the filamentous blanket or silkweed, a particular problem where ponds are unbalanced (*see* Chapter 3). The best way to remove it is to take a strong piece of wood, twist it around simultaneously rotating it throughout the pond.

There are various proprietary treatments for clearing water available, which work upon different principles such as microscopic filtration or precipitation. These can be used with confidence, but – as with all such products – it is important to read the instructions carefully and only to use as directed.

AUTUMN

Shortening days and lower temperatures mean that all forms of life are beginning to slow down in preparation for the winter. The water garden is still beautiful and the lilies seem to acquire a final burst of energy to give the last blaze of colour, brilliant in the autumn. But as the season progresses, there will be fewer flowers and amphibians will have sought wet stones and other sites where they can spend the winter. Gather the seeds of any marginals or other plants required for sowing in the spring.

Overwintering

Tropical and other tender subjects such as water-hyacinths, water-chestnuts and tender fish should be brought inside into an aquarium for the winter. Where it is likely that leaves will enter the pond through falling from a nearby tree or as a result of

A general view of a water garden in late summer; the dead heads should be removed before winter.

being carried long distances by autumnal gales, cover the pond with netting. The first frosts will turn the leaves of the marginals black; these should be removed before they have a chance to enter the water.

GATHERING OF SEEDS

1. Wait until the seed pods have turned light brown in colour, or in the case of berries until they are soft to the touch. Whilst it is important to wait until the seeds are ripe, unnecessary delays must be avoided as they will self-disperse or may be eaten by birds or other animals.
2. Pick the stalk complete with seed pods or berries. If this is not practical, the pods themselves may be gathered directly.
3. Stand the seed pods on a piece of paper on the shelf of the greenhouse.
4. Separate the seeds from their cases, or from the fleshy berries. Place them on a piece of kitchen towel and stand on the windowsill until dry.
5. Place in a clearly marked envelope and store in a cool dry room until they are needed for sowing the following spring.

As soon as the vegetation of the Gunnera has died down, use it to cover the crown of the plant. This should be sufficient to protect the slightly tender subject through the cold months ahead. Alternatively, protect with a layer of straw.

WINTER

During the winter months, organic materials will continue to decompose on the floor of the pond, resulting in the build up of the gases methane, ammonia and hydrogen sulphide. At the same time the fish will be using the oxygen dissolved in the water. It is essential that even during the severest spells of cold weather, an exchange of gases can take place and that at least a small surface area is kept clear of ice. The easiest way of achieving this is to place a ball on the surface of the pond. Slight currents and the wind will cause the ball to move about, and this movement will be sufficient to stop the water in a small area from freezing. This alone will be effective in milder areas in all but the severest of winters, but there will always be occasions when the water freezes even around the ball. Such frosts will take many hours, even days, to thaw and urgent action must be taken if the lives of the fish are to be saved! An ice hole should be opened immediately: for this you will need a very large tin can, the larger the better, and one or more jugs of near-boiling water. Place the can as far towards the centre of the pond as you can safely reach from the edge and pour in the boiling water until the can heats up and melts a hole in the ice. Never attempt to break the ice with a hammer or other means as the blows will set up compression waves which will

kill the fish! Similarly, boiling water poured directly on to the ice will cause shock to the fish below the surface.

Prevention is better than cure and this can be achieved by ensuring that the pond does not freeze over in the first place. This is done by using one of the small purpose-built pond heaters connected to the mains supply. They are not designed to raise the temperature of the whole pond, only a small area sufficient for the necessary exchange of gases to take place. It is not necessary to keep the heater on throughout the winter; it need only be switched on when frosts are imminent. Hard frosts usually occur on clear nights in mid-winter when there is no cloud cover.

Remember to maintain a water garden during winter.

CHAPTER 8

Indoor Water Gardens

As gardens have become progressively smaller, we have taken them more and more into our homes. A century ago the only subject that was grown inside was the humble pot plant, the ubiquitous aspidistra, but today indoor gardening has become an art. Each year plans become more and more ambitious, with indoor ponds in conservatories, large aquaria in which a wide range of plants including an increasing number of tropical wetland subjects are grown. If these are to prosper indoors they should be treated as bogland subjects, and the ideal humidity created, otherwise they will die. The range of wetland subjects is enormous. A small selection is described below, but the list is by no means exhaustive. For example, the orchids have been left out as being far too specialist for a general treatment. Included are examples of insectivorous plants, which extract nutrients from the bodies of flies and other insects that they trap to supplement the virtually nutrient-deficient soils, and ferns, once very popular with our Victorian ancestors, which are enjoying a renaissance. These primitive plants, direct descendants of the world of the dinosaurs, are true wetland subjects and are worthy of their place in any indoor or outdoor water garden. The choice is almost limitless, and the indoor gardener's problem is in choosing what to omit rather than what to include.

Few aspects of horticulture can offer so much pleasure, or so much interest as the water garden, and it is a feature that may be created in any house, irrespective of its size or position.

Changing architectural styles and ways of life have completely revolutionized the use of plants in interior decoration. Flat-dwellers, and those living in properties with little or no garden, can create gardens inside to compensate for the lack of greenery outside. In the heart of the cities are to be found an increasing number of cultivated plants, the majority growing inside properties. The growing of exotic subjects such as the tropical waterlilies was once considered beyond the pocket of all but the wealthiest but today, with central heating and a little care, the majority of subjects can be

The narrow-leaved marsh orchid, Dactylorhiza traunsteineri.

Water-lilies are of course vital to the layout of a water garden.

grown in most living areas. Landings and other communal areas of flats are now being internally landscaped; many properties incorporate a conservatory, where the indoor water garden is a leading contender for space. The traditional collection of pot plants is no longer sufficient for the modern indoor gardener.

INDOOR PONDS

Indoor ponds will of necessity be smaller than those generally encountered outside. The most practical method of construction is to use a fibreglass liner although, since the danger of frost damage will be completely eliminated, a concrete pond with appropriate sealer is equally effective. Since

there is no danger of weather damage, raised ponds present no problems and represent one of the best approaches to most internal landscaping designs. They are also especially suitable when designing gardens for the handicapped.

With all indoor water systems some ancillary heating additional to that afforded by the central heating system must be provided. The central heating system creates a temperature above the water in which the flowers can open naturally. If the ambient temperature is not high enough, the blooms will not open properly and will fail to emit their true perfume. This failure to provide the necessary heat often leads to disappointing results when attempting to grow tropicals. The usual way of growing these plants is to plant them out during the spring to have them flowering during the summer, when the central heating is not working. However, there is no specific reason why they should be grown in this way. Many of the subjects originate from the southern hemisphere, and winter flowering is natural. In the tropics, seasons tend to be far less pronounced, and the plants will bloom all the year round. You can have some of your plants flowering whenever you choose, providing you take sufficient care to provide the correct level of light intensity – the main factor affecting the growth of plants. This may involve the provision of artificial lighting. The flowering of water-lilies depends to some extent upon the intensity of sunlight, but in this case increasing the length of time of exposure to light beyond the natural amount will only increase the vegetative growth; it will not extend the flowering time, which is fixed genetically.

Indoor water gardening considerably extends the range of plants which can be cultivated. For example, there are heaters designed for outside ponds which will effectively extend the flowering season and allow for the successful growth of the near-hardy subjects such as the water hyacinth, but they are not totally successful with most of the tropical water-lilies. The latter, which include some of the most beautiful members of the genus, must be in a much more friendly environment, and an indoor water garden allows you to do this.

THE AQUARIUM

The use of indoor aquaria to house tropical and cold water fish has long been established, but equally effective results can be achieved when plants are grown in them. Often the only reason for this type of container's failure is that it is too small. Best results are achieved by using an aquarium of at least 4ft (120cm) in length. It is essential to appreciate that the base on which such containers are sited is very important. An aquarium of 4 × 2½ × 3ft (120 × 75 × 90cm), filled to within 2–3in (5–7.5cm) of the top, will contain ¾ ton of water. Such a structure needs a brick or concrete foundation. Whilst aquaria of such size tend to be more expensive than ponds, they have a considerable advantage in that it is possible to raise fish *and* observe them. By including both animal and plant life it is possible to create a totally tropical pool environment. Combining both tropical fish and plants requires special techniques. With the fish aquarium it is usual to provide a hood, where the lighting is situated, and which reduces heat losses. Due to the height of many of the marginal plants it is not always possible to use a hood, and in this case other systems of lighting must be considered.

The ideal temperature for a true tropical aquarium is 75°F (23.5°C). This is higher than the comfortable living temperature which is maintained on the average central heating system, and for the best results with the fish it is advisable to fit a thermostatically controlled heater. These are cheap to buy – in terms of the benefit you will gain from the slight rise in temperature that you are seeking to maintain, the cost is negligible.

Far less oxygen will dissolve in the warm water than in the cold water aquarium, and to maintain the necessary oxygen level you will need to fit a small air pump. These may be obtained cheaply from any tropical fish supplier. It is advisable to incorporate a filter with the air pump in order to maintain clear water throughout the system.

ESTABLISHING THE INDOOR GARDEN

Whether you opt for a pond or aquarium, and warm or cool conditions, the procedure for setting up remains basically the same. The only point to note is that with the aquarium much more attention must be paid to the visual effect from the side.

FERNS AND RELATED PLANTS SUITABLE FOR GROWING INDOORS

Adiantum capillus veneris (maidenhair fern)
Asparagus plumosus (florist fern)
Asplenium bulbiferum
Ceterach offinicarum
Nephrolepis Exaltata
Phyllitis scolopendrium vulgare (hart's tongue)
Platycerium bifurcatum
Pteris cretica
Seleginella apus

Since the position will be permanent, it is possible to some extent to deceive the eye; flower pots and other containers may be concealed behind rocks so that they appear to be part of the natural scene. Plants grown in containers can be removed from time to time in order to replant or prune back the growths – the restricted size of the indoor structure means that the size of any individual plant can attain is greatly reduced. Those plants to be to the front of the aquarium must be growing naturally, and this may be best achieved by placing 1in (2.5cm) of peat on the floor of the container, followed by 1½in–2in (3–5cm) of pea gravel.

PLANTS FOR HEATED POOL OR AQUARIUM

Water-lilies

As with plants for outside water gardens, the most spectacular is the water-lily. It is magnificent in form, with a marvellous scent, and it is well worth considering growing it as a solitary subject apart from the indoor pool. You can do this by growing the plant in an old wooden beer or cider barrel which has been cut in two. Such containers are readily fitted with an aquarium heater and are the equivalent of a flower pot, with the water-lily as the pot plant growing in the water medium. As with hardy specimens, the lilies should not be planted until the spring. Where tub planting is involved the rhizomes are planted into a rich potting medium, while in a large heated pool the method of planting is as for the temperate varieties.

Nelumbium

Nelumbiums or sacred lotuses are very similar to water-lilies. They are far less well known than the *Nymphaea*, probably because there are no true hardy forms. The leaves, which tend to be very dramatic, are borne on stems which can be from 6–8ft (2–2.5m) in height. The rhizome should be planted in early spring in about 12in (30cm) of water, or even in a pot, providing the soil is always submerged. Unlike the water-lily, the majority of the growth is above the water and these may be con-

sidered as tropical marginals. The roots are lifted and stored in a dry place during the winter.

Two species are cultivated – *N. lutea*, which has globe-shaped yellow flowers 6–8in (15–20cm) across, and *N. nucifera*, which has pinkish-red flowers of a similar size.

Panama Pacific is a vigorous-growing hybrid which deepens its colour as it ages. It is a strong grower but only requires about 2ft (60cm) of water.

Eichhornia (Water-hyacinth)

These may be cultivated outside during the summer months, provided that they are brought into the warm in early autumn. The rhizomes may be planted in the aquarium during the spring in a leafy compost. (Those to be grown in the outside pond should be treated in the same manner and transplanted outside into leafy compost only when there is no longer any danger of frost.) The pale pinkish-blue flowers appear about three months after planting.

THE INDOOR WET GARDEN

There is no need to build an indoor wet garden in the way that one is specially prepared outside. Set aside a separate part of the conservatory especially for growing these damp land plants. Lay a large, shallow, metal tray, and over this place a layer of gravel, which must be kept permanently moist. The plants can then be grown individually in pots resting on the gravel.

Wetland plants suitable for growing indoors originate from two distinct sources: natural bogs and tropical rainforests. In the latter, they often grow on decaying leaves trapped in the canopy high above the forest floor – not true bog plants at all, but since both require similar conditions it is convenient to grow them together in the same environment.

Requirements of Wetland Plants Grown Indoors

1. They must have the correct temperature: 50–70°F (10–21°C) is suitable for all of the species recommended in this text.
2. They must be kept constantly moist.

WATER-LILIES FOR THE INDOOR POOL

SPECIES

N. amazona A very large white-flowered species, with blooms up to 4in (10cm) across. It has a heavy seductive scent.

N. capensis This has a bright blue green foliage, but little scent. It grows in 1–2ft (30–60cm) of water.

N. caerulea Known as the Egyptian blue lotus. Delicate pale blue flowers 6–8in (15–20cm) across. Grows best in 2ft (60cm) of water.

N. colorata Although the flowers are only about 1in (2.5cm) across, it is popular due to the delicate lilac blue colour of the flowers. Requires 1½–2ft (45–60cm) of water.

N. mexicana Bright yellow flowers of 3–4in (7–10cm) across. Requires 3ft (1m) of water.

N. lotus One of the largest of all of the species, with flowers over 6in (15cm) across, yet only requires 2–2½ft (60–75cm) of water. Sweetly scented.

N. stellata Blue star-shaped flowers with golden yellow stamens. Requires 2ft (60cm) of water. A spectacular subject, ideal for growing in barrels.

HYBRIDS

African Gold One of the miniature water-lilies suitable for growing in the aquarium, needing only 12in (30cm) of water. It has buttercup-yellow flowers.

Blue Beauty One of the most startling of all water-lily hybrids, with a cup of blue petals encasing a golden centre with purple stamens. Only suitable for larger ponds as it requires 3–4ft (90–120cm) of water.

General Pershing Amongst the most dramatic of all water-lilies with very large pink flowers which open over 12in (30cm) above the water. It can be grown in 3ft (1m) of water, although it prefers extra depth.

James Guerney Heavily scented flowers of over 8in (20cm) across. It has very deep pink petals and reddish-yellow stamens, and needs about 3ft (90cm) of water. A night-flowering hybrid.

Missouri Another night-flowering variety, said to have flowers sometimes as much as 18in (45cm) across, although they are usually a little smaller than this. The brilliant white blooms are held above the water.

3. They require the correct compost: most will grow in a mixture of equal parts sharp sand and peat.
4. They must be regularly fed: with any proprietary pot-plant food throughout the growing season. For those plants that do not have a resting period, give half strength feed once a fortnight.

Bromeliads

A large group of plants originating from central and South America. They grow in a range of habitats, some in quite dry locations. It is a very diverse group, which includes the pineapple, but we are concerned only with those that grow in very damp locations: in marshy ground or damp decaying leaves high in the forest canopy.

Bromeliads tend to have shallow roots, which allows even mature plants to be grown in a maximum of 6–8in (15–20cm) pots. The characteristic feature of all bromeliads is that their leaves are often leathery with sharp protective spikes, arranged in rosettes. These often form water-tight structures which trap and hold rainwater. In the wilds of the rainforests, land frogs often lay their eggs in this reservoir, which then becomes home for their tadpoles – the ideal subject for inclusion in any indoor water garden.

BROMELIAD GENERA

These are essentially indoor plants which can be grown in conjunction with an internal aquascape. They tend to grow in moist conditions, and it is the fogs and mists of the rainforest in which they are at home. In many instances their shallow roots take hold in the general plant detritus which collects in the branch joints and the crevices of the bark. These plants have formed cup-like structures as a result of necessary modifications, trap and retain moisture and should also be kept damp, but not soaked.
Aechmea
Billbergia
Cryptanthus
Neoregelia
Vriesia

BROMELIADS

Several species readily available from garden centres.
Description The characteristic feature is the leaves, which are long, lanceolate, and arranged in rosettes. The true flowers often insignificant, but usually surrounded by brightly coloured bracts which combine to form a spectacular florescence.
Flowering period Throughout the year, depending upon species and cultural conditions. The coloured bracts may last for several months.
Cultivation Plant in a mixture of equal parts sharp sand and loam. Maintain the temperature at 59–69°F (15–20°C). Water freely with species such as the urn plant, which has a large reservoir: maintain about 1in (2cm) of water in the hollow. This is often the part from which the flower emerges.
Propagation Small rosettes will grow at the base of the plant. These should be allowed to remain for at least a full season. During the summer, remove the plant from the pot and cut through the roots with a sharp knife severing the young plant from the parent.

Bromeliads are grown for their very large and colourful bracts which may remain for up to six months; the true flowers are smaller, insignificant and far shorter-lived.

Cryptocoryne

These species are of eastern origin, and are members of the arum family. They tend not to be as popular in the UK as they are in mainland Europe, and can only be obtained from specialist suppliers; nevertheless, they are intriguing conservatory subjects. They may be grown as wetland subjects providing that their soil is kept constantly sodden. They are not difficult plants, but the success with which you are able to grow them will depend upon the depth of the water and its temperature, which should be about 60°F (15°C). They prefer semi-shaded conditions.

For the beginner, *C. becketti*, the smallest of all the cultivated cryptocorynes, grows well as a hot-house marginal. Its only requirement is that its roots are constantly submerged. It is free flowering but is valued as much for its foliage as its florescence.

C. cordota, another popular species, prefers moist soils to being totally submerged. Larger species suited for cultivation include *C. willissii* and *C. ciliata*, which may have leaves up to 8in (20cm) in length.

Drosera (The Sundews)

These insectivorous plants grow naturally in bogs and are ideal conservatory subjects. Being mainly of European origin they are not hothouse subjects, but they do need to be grown inside, where their special requirements may be provided for.

The leaves are covered with red thickened hairs, at the end of which is a sticky fluid which entraps the small insects; that are attracted towards them, believing that that are a source of nectar. The struggles of the entrapped insects stimulates the hairs to bend towards the leaves. These then secrete digestive juices which extract the minerals from the victim. In the impoverished boglands which are the natural home to these curious plants, this is the only way that they can obtain the nitrogen and other minerals that they require. The peaty soil in which they live is deplete of virtually all nutrients, and they prefer a slightly acid soil.

Propagation of these plants is best achieved through the separation of the new plantlets. Plant the new stock in peat – under no circumstances place fertilizer in the compost or attempt to feed the plants as this will probably kill them.

There are over one hundred species of sundew. Amongst the commonest in cultivation are *D. angelica* or greater sundew, a plant of the heathlands, and *D. rotundifolia*. Both are low growing, the leaves varying from ½–1½in (1–4cm) with insignificant flowers of less than 1in (2.5cm) across.

Eucharis

This is a member of the amaryllis family and is not usually considered as a water garden subject. However, it does require considerably more moisture than the other members of the genus, and only prospers in wetland conditions. The bulbs, available only from specialist suppliers, should be planted during the spring. Like all members of the amaryllis family it is characterized by trumpet-like flowers which tend to form in clusters.

E. grandiflora is the largest eucharis, with leaves up to 10in (25cm) in length. *E. korsakovii* is the dwarf eucharis, whose leaves seldom grow to more than 4in (10cm) long. Both species need a steady temperature of 60°F (15°C). Your choice should depend purely on the space available.

Kaempferia

These are natural wetland plants that require a very humid atmosphere and will only thrive where this can be created. They have small delicate flowers, faintly reminiscent of the solanums, and rich green leaves which create an almost hosta-like foliage. They perform a similar role in the indoor water garden to that of the hosta outside.

K. pulchra has 6in (15cm) long leaves and is the most suitable species for medium-sized water gardens. *K. rotunda* is twice the size of *K. pulchra*, and is only suitable for the larger indoor water garden. Where room allows it can provide a spectacular accompaniment to the other subjects. Both are cultivated from rhizomes which should be planted in a humus-rich compost during the spring. Being tropical in origin, they require a constant temperature of 65–70°F (18.5–21°C).

Sarracenia (The Pitcher Plant)

Carnivorous plants are never easy subjects to grow, but the pitcher plants are amongst the most successful in cultivation. The leaves are modified to form an urn or pitcher shape. This holds a liquid which attracts insects by its smell of decaying flesh. Once inside the pitcher they end up trapped in the liquor which contains digestive juices. These extract the minerals that the plant needs from the body of the insect. Pitcher plants may be grown from seed sown in peat compost during the early spring. The growing medium must never be allowed to dry out and the plants should not be fed. Plant the young seedlings individually into pots and transfer the pots to the shallow end of the pond or aquarium. Being of temperate origin (they all come from North America), they may be transferred to the outside wet garden during the summer months. It is essential to ensure that they are not allowed to dry out during this period. Bring them inside in early autumn and keep in a frost-free area. Watering may be reduced during the winter months.

Ferns

Primitive in form, the fern is a true wetland species. There are several species which are temperate, and which can be grown completely satisfactorily outside, but they are usually cultivated indoors as a pot plant. Ferns will survive with very little more moisture than is provided by regular watering, but they do need water for their curious mode of reproduction. The plant kingdom is divided into flowering and non-flowering species, with ferns belonging to the second category. Since they have no flowers, they use a means of reproduction which dates back to the days of the primaeval forests.

The fern consists of a root, often filamentous and providing little anchorage, stems and fronds. The fronds perform the main function of leaves in the higher plants, in that they generate food and produce spores. When ripe, spores fall from the fronds onto the moist soil. In time they germinate to form a plant that is dissimilar to the parent, called a prothallus. it is this plant which then produces the gametes. If there is sufficient water present, the male sex cell projects itself, by means of its whip-like cilia, to fertilise the female ovum. The new structure germinates and the intermediate prothallus, its role now complete, dies.

It is possible to purchase the spores of ferns, which will germinate to form the prothalluses, and if there is sufficient moisture they will produce the desired forms. Growing ferns in this way can be one of the most rewarding and satisfying of gardening experiences, but you must be patient. It often takes two years to produce new plants in this way. The more usual way of propagating the stock is to divide the crowns of the plants. As with all vegetative propagation this is most successful if accomplished during the spring.

There are several different fern species and related plants. For a detailed description a specialist book should be consulted.

Ferns kept indoors should be regularly sprayed to keep them moist.

CHAPTER 9

Propagation

Plants may be propagated by one of two methods, either sexual (with seeds or spores) or vegetative. A new plant that has been propagated vegetatively will be a clone generated from just one parent; a plant propagated from seed or spores will be the result of male and female gametes combining together, so it will possess the qualities of two parents. The seeds from many of the new hybrid varieties do not germinate to produce offspring identical to their parents; often the flower – the most important part from the gardener's point of view – is totally unpredictable. It is only the species, those forms which have emerged in the wild, and others which have had the time and opportunity for their genes to settle down, that produce seedlings identical to their parents. Unless you are sure that the varieties you wish to grow will germinate true from seeds you should limit your propagation by seeds to species. When two species are crossed they produce seedlings different from either parent and it is this which has resulted in the emergence of superior forms. In order to maintain the same gene pattern and desired characteristics it is necessary to reproduce these cultivars vegetatively.

If you intend to propagate plants on any more than the occasional basis it is essential to set aside part of the water garden as a nursery area, as you would with terrestrial subjects.

VEGETATIVE METHODS OF REPRODUCTION

There are natural methods of vegetative reproduction, which occur as a result of the ability of plant cells (before they are fully formed) to adapt and reproduce themselves to form root cells and hence new plants. The gardener can use this natural process to his own needs, and help it by stimulating the cells to form root cells. There will always be some tendency to do this wherever cells are cut or damaged, but in some instances the plant will die before life-supporting roots can be established. Aquatic subjects, which can take their nutrients through various parts of the system, are often more readily propagated by these means. Growth is stimulated by

Poolside planting is left to right: Acer palmatum, Polygonum amplexicaule atrosanguineum *and* Iris pallida variegata.

hormones and the greatest concentration of these will, for all practical purposes, lie at the axil joints where the secondary buds form. Cuttings should always be taken just below axil joints and any leaves removed. The division of cells will depend upon both the temperature and the length of daylight and so cuttings and divisions should be performed in the spring or early summer as is practical.

Self Sets

These are new plants which form at some distance from the parent and are the result of a shoot developing and growing from one of the extremities of the root. The new plants are removed and this is the simplest of all methods of propagation, although it has the disadvantage that it will lead to the pool becoming quickly overgrown by the colonizing species.

Cuttings

All water plants with elongated leaf axil joints may be propagated by means of cuttings. Your knife must be sharp, as blunt instruments can lead to damage of several cells within the vicinity of the cut, and rotting diseases setting in.

With all water plants it is better to delay transplanting rooted cuttings to the permanent site until they are quite large; this ensures that they will remain at the bottom of the pool. This is particularly important as they do tend to be deep rooted, and will only overcome buoyancy through saturation of the tissues in the water. This only occurs when the plants are sufficiently well developed.

Division

Crown Division

Plants with crowns have compacted leaf axil joints, and the best way to propagate them is through division of the crowns. Lift a large plant, then place two forks (hand forks for small plants, ordinary garden forks for large crowns) back to back at its centre. Divide the crown into two by pulling the two forks apart. Whether the new plants are aquatic or terrestrial it is best to place the divisions in a flower pot with John Innes No. 2 or similar compost and allow them to establish roots before they are placed into their permanent site.

TAKING CUTTINGS STEP-BY-STEP

1. Fill a flower pot with compost made up of one part peat, one part well-rotted cow manure, and one part sharp sand or fine gravel. Remove 2in (5in) long growing tips from the parent plant using a clean, sharp knife. Remove the base leaves from each cutting so that only two remain.

2. Place the cuttings around the edge of a flower pot – for some reason rooting seems easier at this position. Place the flower pot in a shallow part of the pond. Leave it until the plants have rooted, then plant them into their permanent positions.

Rhizome Division

Water-lilies have rhizomes, which lend themselves to division. These should be lifted in the spring and cut into pieces about 4in (10cm) long with a sharp knife. The pieces are planted into the pool in the same way that you would plant the particular species. Many roots show several eyes, but it is advisable to reduce these to no more than three. The weaker or secondary buds will only form inferior growths which will reduce the vigour of the main shoots.

SEEDS

It is well known that terrestrial plants differ considerably in their germination periods and the size of their various seeds. Information is less readily available concerning the germination of water plants. In nature the ripe seeds fall from the parent and may be carried a considerable distance before they settle and germinate. This usually involves over-wintering in the natural environment. Such methods are wasteful and, where there is only a limited seed supply, greater control over the germination is required.

Gather the seeds when they are ripe and store them in a dry place until the following spring. This

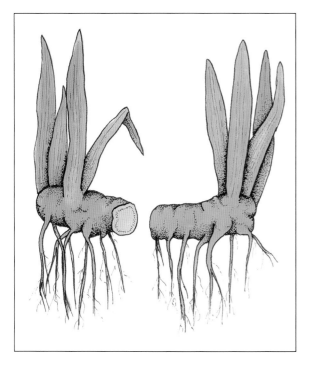

Rhizome division; cut with a sharp knife and ensure that there are no jagged edges where disease can set in.

SOWING SEEDS STEP-BY-STEP

1. Prepare an aquarium and fill it two-thirds full with water. Fill small flower pots with germinating compost.

2. Where the seeds are too small to handle individually, mix them thoroughly with a large quantity of white sand and sow the mixture on to the surface of the compost. This will ensure an even distribution of seeds. Where large seeds are sown, cover only very lightly with sand. If the seedlings rise to the surface once germination has taken place, allow them to sink – this will occur when the modified stem structure has had the opportunity to become full of water.

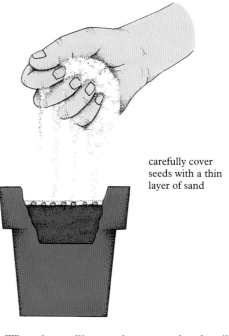

carefully cover seeds with a thin layer of sand

3. When the seedlings are large enough to handle, replant them in pots filled with growing compost, and allow them to remain in the aquarium until they are large enough for transplanting into their permanent positions.

may seem unnatural but it does eliminate the danger of rotting. No germination will take place until the temperature is sufficiently high, so delay planting until mid- to late spring. It is essential to be able to see the seeds without disturbing them.

Germination of Seedlings

Although wetland plants require or can tolerate damp conditions, more seeds and seedlings are lost from damping off than from insufficient moisture. There are two classes of annuals – the hardy variety, which can tolerate frosts, and the half-hardy subjects, which cannot. With all annuals it is important that the young plants are available to be transplanted into their final positions when there is no longer any danger of frosts; this will be late May or June in most areas of the UK. A good early start is essential if the plants are to reach their full potential. The exact planting date will depend upon the species, but many must be started as early as late winter or early spring.

At this time of year it is necessary to provide external heat to bring about germination. This can easily be achieved in any house by use of a small electrically heated propagating unit.

To raise the contents of an average packet of seeds, half-fill a small margarine tub with sowing compost, and then sprinkle the seed evenly over the surface. (Mix very small seeds with sand, as before.) The depth to which seeds must be planted will depend upon their size. Large seeds can produce sprouts that are long enough to push up through the soil, before the plant can support itself by photosynthesis. The seeds of these plants should be sown at a sufficient depth to ensure that they have adequate anchorage.

Some seeds, on the other hand, like those of the begonias, are so small that they can hardly be seen by the naked eye. They contain such a small food supply that the plants must be self-supporting from the moment that the sprout bursts through the seed coat. They should not be covered with any soil or they will perish before they have had the chance to emerge through the soil.

Cover the container with paper until the majority of the seeds have germinated, then remove the paper and allow the seedlings to develop in full day-

Ferns can be propagated by division, but it might be more rewarding to try growing them from spores.

light. This daylight is very important. If there is insufficient light, the seedlings will be drawn up towards what is available and they will tend to be spindly. The secret of successful seedling raising is to ensure that you achieve strong green growth, rather than the thin weak greenery that is the sign of poor management. When the seeds are about 1in (2–3cm) in length, and are just beginning to show their second pair of leaves, they should be pricked out into a seed box containing growing compost. A standard-sized seed box will hold forty-eight plants in eight rows of six. With the larger subjects such as salvias, which make a most dramatic statement around the pond during the summer months, it is better to plant only half this quantity.

Allow the plants to grow to three-quarters of the size they should be for planting out – 3–4in (7–10cm). With half-hardy annuals you will need to provide some heat during this stage and, if you only have a few plants (perhaps enough for a small town garden), they may be grown on in a propagator. For larger quantities a cool greenhouse or even a windowsill will be suitable for the short period of

PROPAGATION OF FERNS STEP BY STEP

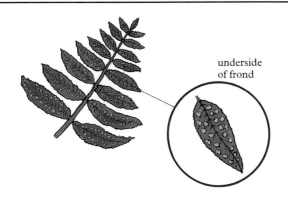

underside
of frond

Spores may be purchased from seedsmen, or gathered. To gather spores:

1. Select a mature frond late in the summer when the spore cases are ripe. Place a piece of newspaper under the frond and tap just above the spore cases. The powder-like spores will be released on to the paper.
2. Ferns require the same conditions to germinate as those that encourage fungal growths, so it is necessary to sterilize the compost to destroy the fungal spores.
3. Prepare a margarine pot by making several holes in the bottom and then covering it with a layer of grit. Add a mixture of equal parts peat and sharp sand to within ½in (1cm) of the top. Pour boiling water through the mixture, then allow it to drain before placing the pot containing the compost inside a polythene bag to cool. Prepare one pot for each species you intend to sow.
4. When the compost has cooled, sow the spores thinly over the surface. Return the container to the polythene bag and secure with a rubber band.
5. Stand in partial shade in a temperature of 59–64°F (15–18°C).

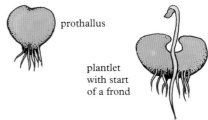

prothallus

plantlet
with start
of a frond

6. Three to four months later, the surface will be covered by flat green vegetation composed of several prothalli. If the polythene bag is secured there will be adequate moisture; if not the container should be stood in a saucer of water until the compost is damp before returning to the bag.
7. Allow to remain until distinct plantlets with fronds have developed, by which time they should be large enough to handle and can be transferred to individual pots.

time that they are at this critical stage. When they are almost at the planting out stage, place the seed boxes in a cold frame and leave the cover off during the daytime. If you do not have a cold frame, simply leave the seedlings outside during the daytime but bring them in at night. Young seedlings are particularly attractive to birds, especially pigeons; if these present a danger, place the young plants under netting during the daytime. As soon as the danger of frosts seems to have passed – use your own judgement and the weather forecasts rather than set dates – set the plants out into their permanent positions.

Germination of Fern Spores

Ferns are primitive non-flowering plants, which do not themselves possess sex organs. Reproduction is by means of spores, powder-like specks found in cases on the underside of the fronds. Native ferns usually produce their spores on mature fronds during mid- and late summer. Spores can be sown like seed when they produce the first stage in their strange life cycle: a flat green structure termed a prothallus. The prothallus is different from the fern itself and may live for a few weeks or, in some cases, several years, depending upon species and environment. The prothallus has only one role, which is to develop male and female organs and to provide a means for fertilization to take place. Its flat surface clinging to the damp ground provides a damp region through which the single male cell can travel to fertilize the female ovary. From this union the new fern – similar in every way to the parent – develops. The prothallus, having fulfilled its role, dies while the young fern develops.

CHAPTER 10

Problems with the Pond

The vast majority of pond owners find that it is a relaxing, trouble-free activity, but problems are, of course, occasionally encountered. It is not unknown for a pond to be trouble free for many years and then begin to develop problems. This will be due presumably to some environmental change which is not readily obvious. Fortunately, most problems may be easily overcome.

WATER PROBLEMS

Green Water

Green-coloured water is produced by the presence of millions of algae, or micro-organisms. You will never completely eradicate algae or stop infection, as the windborne unicellular plant is endemic, but you can ensure that the conditions are not conducive to its growth. It should be considered as a problem which is never solved, but rather as something which must be kept under constant control. A balanced pond life will ensure that there are enough predators effectively to contain the numbers of algae to manageable proportions. Algae require an abundance of mineral salts and light and therefore a large surface area. Where there are sufficient plants, particularly water-lilies, these will absorb the minerals through their stems, and their leaves will simultaneously reduce the surface area through which the light can penetrate. Until the plant growth has established itself you will never completely solve the problem. Dosage with algaecides will produce only a temporary respite; reinfection will soon occur, and a long-term solution should be sought.

Green water may occur immediately after a pond has been cleaned out, when the water-lilies have been thinned, or during the spring before the annual growth of water-lilies has taken place. A fresh supply of compost to the roots or the addition of fertilizer tablets can also cause the problem. Often it is a combination of more than one of these, and it will clear itself.

An example of a healthy water garden with attractive poolside planting.

Beware! The pond holds attractions for a variety of unwelcome forms of life including scum-like algae. A spring-clean is essential if this is not to detract from the beauty.

Black Water

This is an extremely dangerous condition, the result of the decomposition of leaves and other plant materials over the winter period, or a build up of detritus because of neglect of the pond over several years. It is most frequently encountered where a pond is situated immediately under a large tree. The only cure is to clean out the pond completely and then re-establish it from the beginning. Ensure that plant material does not have the opportunity to enter during future years by putting netting over the pond during the autumn, and regularly cutting back the water weeds.

WEEDS

Blanketweed

This is a green filamentous weed also called silk-weed, which will rapidly spread over the whole of the surface of the pond. The best method for the removal of blanketweed is described on page 44.

Duckweed

Although it is no problem in small amounts, once it has become established this floating two-leaved plant multiplies rapidly and if left unchecked will soon cover the whole pond. It is very difficult to eradicate, but the majority can be easily removed by skimming the surface if the water with a cheap butterfly net, or even a piece of old net curtain stretched across a wire hoop.

STRUCTURAL PROBLEMS

Loss of Water

Any sudden loss of water will be due to damage, either to the bottom or the sides of the pond. This can occur as a result of the action of ice during the winter, through physical damage by a sharp instrument, or because of a flint near the membrane penetrating the liner. The greatest care must be taken to ensure that the skin is not broken for, although most ponds can be repaired, it is a time-consuming process necessitating the complete re-establishment of the system.

REPAIRING PONDS

Remove fish and plants completely, then drain the pond.

Repairing Concrete Ponds

1. Thoroughly clean the area around the crack with a wire brush.
2. Force concrete into the crack and cover the surface around the fissure with a thin layer of concrete, smoothing with a trowel.
3. Cover the repaired area with pond paint to ensure that it is watertight and to reduce the danger of toxins being leached out of the water.

Repairing Fibreglass Ponds

Fibreglass consists of glass embedded in a plastic resin and it is the resin which must be repaired.

A large pool covered in duckweed.

1. Having drained the pond, remove the debris and clean the pond with washing-up liquid.
2. Dry thoroughly.
3. Repair the damage with one of the special resin repair kits.

Repairing Plastic Liners

Tears in a plastic liner usually result from contact with a sharp instrument, which may occur either as the membrane is stretched through pressure, or through accidental piercing. The liner is repaired by patching, using a special kit available from the water garden centres.

1. Drain the pond and remove the debris.
2. Clean the surface of the liner with washing-up liquid.
3. Ensure that the area is dry, and dust with talcum powder.
4. Using a suitable adhesive, cover the hole with a piece of the same material from which the liner was made. If it is impossible to obtain the correct material, it will be necessary to remove a piece from the edge of the liner.

Butyl-rubber liners

These are repaired by means of special self-adhesive tape obtainable from your water garden suppliers.

FISH

The fish that are recommended are hardy and can withstand the rigours of the British climate, providing they enjoy a suitable environment. However, from time to time they do experience problems.

Fish floating on its back As many people who have kept goldfish in a bowl will tell you, salt is almost a cure-all with these fish. When fish are observed in a distressed state, place them in an aquarium with salt at the rate of a teaspoonful per gallon (4.5 litres). This will often revive them.

White cotton-like growths on body or fins This is due to a fungal infection and must be treated as soon as it is observed, otherwise it will spread rapidly throughout the whole body. Generally it is associated with a fish which has become damaged, especially just after the winter's fast when its resistance to infection is at its lowest. Various proprietary treatments are available for adding to the water. Since the problem is associated with the fish being in a generally low condition, it is advisable to treat all your fish, irrespective of whether symptoms are visible or not.

Rot of extremities and body blemishes These symptoms cover the whole range of tissue-wasting signs which are common for a variety of diseases and are the result of bacterial infections. The treatment is to apply a bacteriacide – available from a water garden supplier – to the pond water. In this way the problem will be solved. If the fish are taken and treated individually without treating the water, the bacteria will remain in the pond to reinfect and attack the healthy fish.

Fish at the surface of the pond, gulping in air Lack of oxygen is the cause of this problem. This

The pond in winter – the best time to effect structural repairs.

may be due to the temperature being too high, to overcrowding or to a combination of the two. Immediate treatment is to remove the fish and place them in a large tank or bath of water. The only long-term solution to this problem (which, if left, will continually recur) is to reduce the number of fish or to provide a pump.

MARAUDERS

Herons

Fortunately this is only a problem for rural pond keepers who live near a river. Herons will soon discover that a pond can provide easy pickings, and the only really effective way to keep them out is to fix 1in (2.5cm) chicken wire over the pond. If this presents a problem a permanent structure must be created which will keep out the herons. This support made from chicken wire or netting can be used to stop the entry of leaves in winter, and will also hold a polythene 'tent' to keep the heat in during the winter.

Cats

This is a far more common problem, as few people live far away from at least one marauding domestic cat. Protect in the same way as for herons.

Insects

Never use pesticides, including organics, on plants growing in or beside ponds as any insecticide entering the water may kill the fish. Even if one application causes no problem, it may build up until it reaches toxic levels. The way to deal with all pests near a pond is to spray them with jets of water. Once in the pond they will provide food for the fish.

Aphids The only insects that are likely to cause problems on marginals are aphids, which can breed very rapidly. These sap-sucking insects reduce the plant's performance by draining its nutrients, often distorting the leaves which may become blanched. The honeydew they secrete feeds a fungus which will soon form black dust over the foliage. This dust – 'sooty mould' – will disappear when the aphids have been removed. In addition to draining the plant's nutrients, aphids spread viral diseases that can cause yellowing or mosaic patterns on leaves, both of which greatly reduce the plant's performance. There is no known cure for viral infections. Because of the rapid increase in numbers and the range of problems which they can produce, it is important that aphids are washed into the water as soon as they are noticed.

Water-lily beetles Water-lily beetles are black, and may be seen on the leaves through the summer. These should not be confused with water beetles and they should be sprayed into the water where

*The grey heron (*Ardea cinerea*). With modern development robbing the heron of its natural habitat it is fast becoming a serious problem in garden pools only taking a few minutes to devour the complete fish stock.*

they will drown and be consumed by the fish.

Caterpillars Caterpillars, usually those of the china-mark moth, will feed on water-lily leaves. These are best dealt with by hand picking. Always wear gloves when picking up any caterpillars or other insects as they can cause skin problems.

Appendices

PLANTS FOR MOIST AREAS AND MARGINS

Gunnera manicata *(above)*.

Aruncus	*Lobelia cardinalis*
Astilbe	*Mimulus*
Caltha palustris	*Primula*
Eupatorium	*Rununculus*
Gunnera	*Thalictrum*
Hosta	*Trollius*
Iris (var.)	

The combination of Primula florinde *and* Iris pallida variegata *produces a pleasing blend of foliage and flowers.*

WATER AND MARGINAL PLANTS

Agonogeton (water hawthorn)
Calla palustris (bog arum)
Caltha palustris (marsh marigold)
Iris kaempferi (iris)
Iris laevigata (iris)
Mentha aquatica (water mint)
Menyanthes trifoliata (bog bean)
Nymphaea sp. (water lily)
Ranunculus lingua (spearwort)
Sagittaria sagittifolia (arrowhead)
Typha minima (reed mace)

Caltha palustris *'Alba' (left)*.

Sagittaria *(arrowhead)*.

ANNUAL, BIENNIAL AND PERENNIAL PLANTS

The following plants can be grown in beds around water gardens for summer displays. Classification of these plants is not an exact science. Antirrhinums are perennials in that they will continue to flower each year if left undisturbed, but they are usually grown as annuals, with new plants raised each spring and the old removed in the autumn.

Ageratum	*Mesembryanthemum*
Alyssum	*Nasturtium*
Antirrhinum	*Nemesis*
Calceolaria	*Nicotiana*
Calendula	Pansy (summer and
Campanula	winter)
Cineraria	*Pelargonium*
Clarkia	*Phlox*
Cosmos	*Primula*
Delphinium	*Salvia*
Godetia	Stocks
Impatiens	*Tagetes*
Lobelia	*Zinnia*

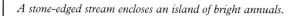

Pelargoniums are a useful bedding plant for added summer interest (above).

A stone-edged stream encloses an island of bright annuals.

DWARF CONIFERS FOR ROCK GARDENS NEAR POOLS

Virtually all dwarf conifers are ideal subjects for growing in conjunction with rocks and water. They should not be grown in sodden soil, but their roots, far shallower than those of the larger species, must be provided with water during the summer months. Amongst the best species and varieties are:

Chamaecyparis obtusa	*Picea abies*
Juniperus horizontalis	*Pinus sylvestris* 'Beuvronensis'

Dwarf conifers make good waterside shrubs and will add interest to a winter bed.

PLANTS FOR A ROCK GARDEN

The following plants may be used in a rock garden built in conjunction with a water garden to provide a range of colour throughout the year.

Alyssum
Arabis
Aricula
Campanula
Cheiranthus
Crane's bill (geranium)
Crocus
Cyclamen (*C. neapolitum*)
Daffodil (miniature)
Dianthus
Gentian
Geum
Helianthemum
Iris reticulata
Narcissus sp. (miniature)
Rhododendron (dwarf species)
Saxifraga
Sedum
Sempervivum
Thyme
Tulip (*kaufmanniana*)

SPRING-FLOWERING BULBS

In some instances there are many different species of these bulbs. Unless otherwise stated, all may be considered as spring-flowering subjects.

Allium (some sp.)
Anemone
Crocus
Daffodil
Hyacinth
Iris (some sp.)
Muscari
Narcissus
Tulips

WATERSIDE TREES AND SHRUBS

Acer palmatum
Azalea
Birch
Box
Cistus
Cotoneaster
Hebe
Magnolia
Malus
Potentilla
Prunus (cherry, plum and almond)
Rosa (some sp.)
Viburnum

Mature shrubs and trees on the water's edge create a natural and secluded atmosphere for the pool.

TERRESTRIAL PLANTS OF MEDIUM HEIGHT

The following plants are useful for growing behind water gardens.

Delphinium
Flag lilies
Foxgloves
Hollyhocks
Lupins (Russell hybrids)
Pampas grass
Red hot pokers

HEATHERS

All heathers may be grown in conjunction with dwarf conifers and rocks as part of the backcloth to a water garden (although some varieties of *Erica carnea* may grow too tall). All heathers require an acid soil; even the so-called 'lime tolerant' varieties fare much better if grown in peat. To create ideal conditions for this plant, remove a quantity of top-soil and replace with peat before planting. Mulch each year with peat. This will be sufficient for these shallow-rooted varieties. The same technique may be used to grow rhododendrons on chalky soils.

WATERSIDE TREES AND SHRUBS

Glossary

Aerobic Normal manner in which organisms respire, breaking down carbohydrates with oxygen to liberate energy.

Anaerobic Respiration without free oxygen; the oxygen contained in the carbohydrate itself is used to liberate the energy, in a far less efficient process than aerobic respiration.

Alpine A rock plant, or appertaining to a rockery.

Batter The angle at which a retaining wall or sloping pond wall is built.

Calyx The collection of sepals in a flower.

Carbohydrate A chemical compound containing carbon, hydrogen and oxygen only. The hydrogen and oxygen are present in the same proportions as in water. This is the material that the plant uses to store its energy (starch), and cellulose, which is necessary to provide mechanical strength.

Cultivar A distinct variety.

Form The height, mass and shape of an organic feature such as a rockery.

Frond The leaf of a fern.

Genus A collection of species which make up a known plant such as a water-lily. Species of the same genus can usually be hybridised. The genus name is the first word in the scientific name, and it is often abbreviated to just the letter where the context is clear. (For example, *Nymphaea* is usually referred to in a list as *N.*, followed by the species name.

Hybrid The cross produced by two species of the same genus, or a cross involving other hybrids.

Inorganic Of mineral origin as opposed to living substances; also to describe man-made chemicals.

Metabolic rate The speed at which energy is used up by a living organism.

Metamorphosis The change of one or more forms of a living organism until the adult form results. Examples include tadpoles changing into frogs, or a caterpillar changing into chrysalis and then into the adult insect.

Microclimate The weather conditions in a very small part of the garden as distinct from the climate in the garden as a whole.

Micro-organism A living thing which is so small that it cannot be seen by the naked eye, although colonies can be seen.

Microbe A contraction of 'micro-organism'.

Mutation A naturally-occurring sport, usually the result of the dominance of a new gene.

Molecule Basic single unit of a chemical compound.

Organic Natural substances (substances which contain carbon).

Oxygen A chemical element capable of releasing stored energy by respiration.

Petal A free segment of the corolla, situated inside the sepals.

pH A scientific scale for comparing the acidity and alkalinity of water. The neutral point is 7.0. Values above are alkaline and those below acidic.

Photosynthesis The process by which plants produce carbohydrates from carbon dioxide and water, using the energy from sunlight.

Plane of symmetry In design, where the feature to the left of a line is related to that to the right in the same way as an object and its mirror image.

Respiration The release of energy within the cells of all living things.

Sepals The outermost component of a flower.

Species A distinct, naturally-occurring form of a genus. The species name is the second word in the scientific name.

Stagnant Still water that is hostile to higher forms of life as a result of decomposing leaves and dissolved materials.

Syn. (synonym) Alternative name

Index